WHAT ABOUT POWER? INQUIRIES INTO CONTEMPORARY SCULPTURE

WHAT ABOUT POWER? INQUIRIES INTO CONTEMPORARY SCULPTURE

SculptureCenter

black dog
publishing
london uk

CONTENTS

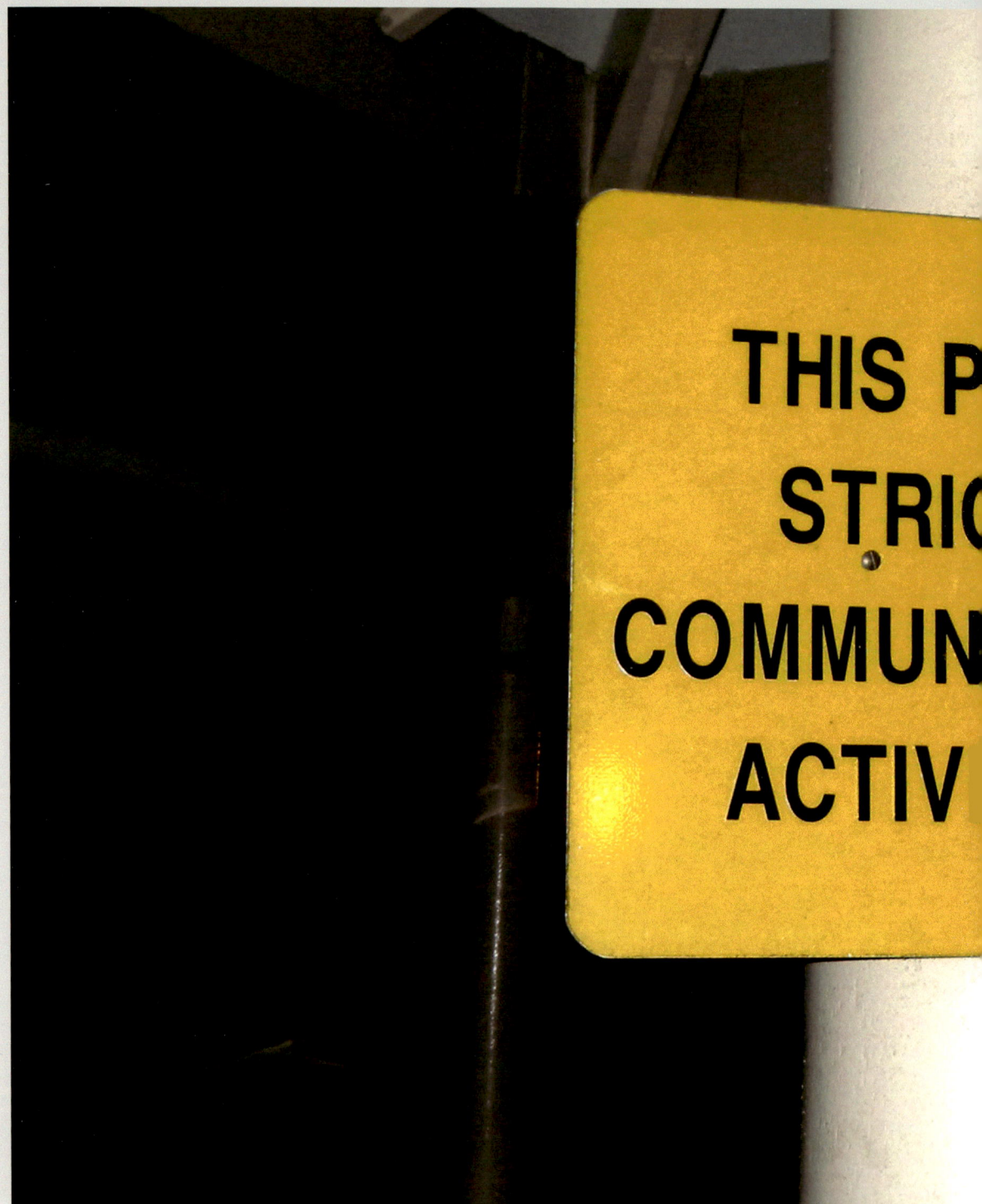

Heman Chong, *This Pavilion is Strictly for Community Bonding Activities Only* from the series *A Short Story About Singapore*, 2014.
Courtesy the artist and Vitamin Creative Space.

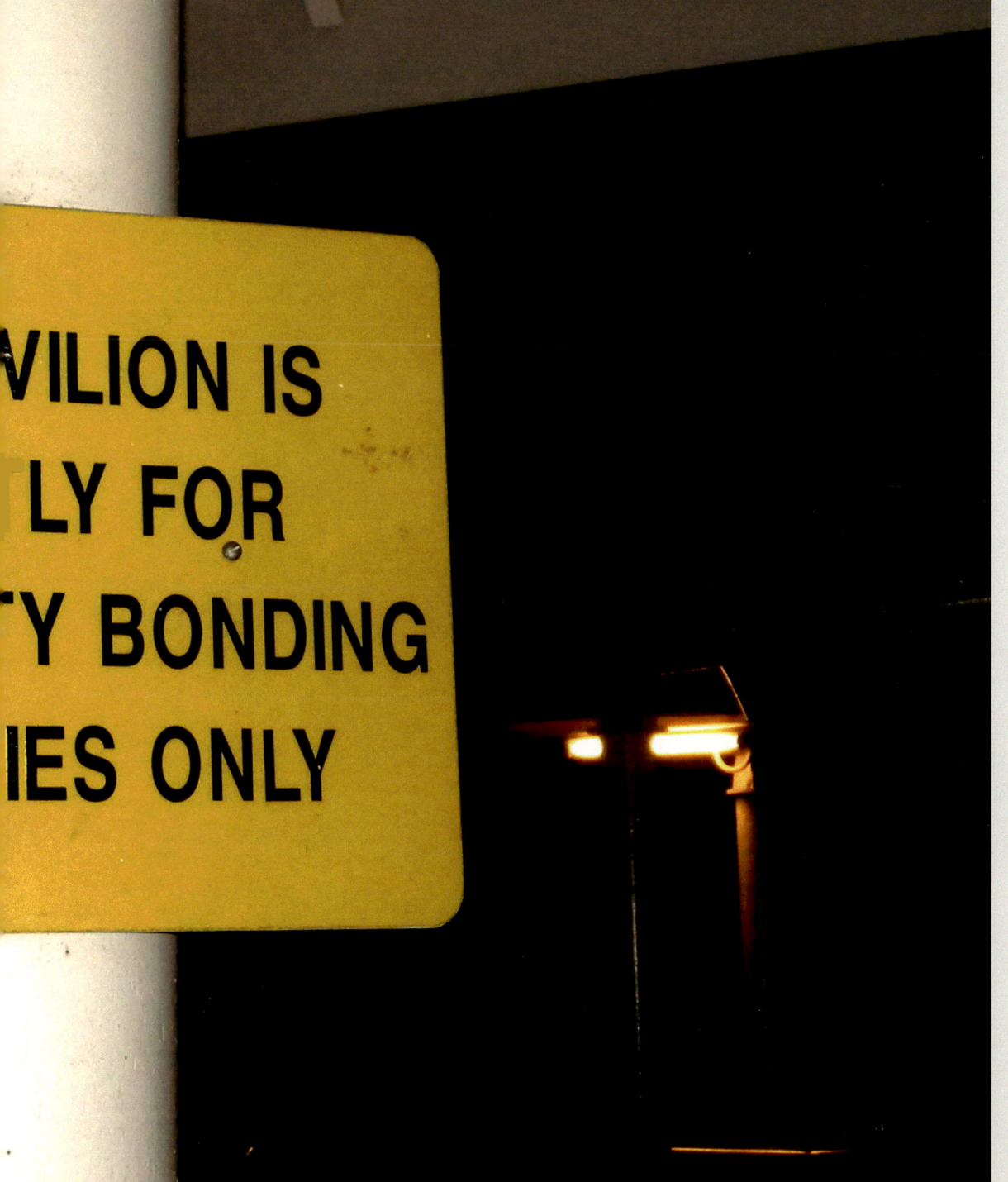

ACKNOWLEDGEMENTS

SculptureCenter launched the *Inquiries into Contemporary Sculpture* series in 2013 to examine the questions and concerns of artists and others working and thinking sculpturally today. SculptureCenter's active and ambitious calendar of programming—including exhibitions, artist commissions, performances and public programs—comprises of a range of investigations and reflects an array of aesthetic strategies and positions. Rejecting a static definition of sculpture, we approach the field of contemporary art with the history and legacy of sculpture as our foundation; a platform from which we can discursively engage artists and audiences around issues of cultural production and meaning. This publication series is an opportunity to think through some of the most pressing concerns of the field both theoretical and practical. The first book in the series, *Where is Production?* considered the increasingly multifaceted modes and sites of production in contemporary sculpture. This volume takes up the question: What is the power dynamic around sculpture today?

Intended to air out some of the most pressing hypotheses and parameters of these inquiries, each book in this series is launched through a daylong gathering of artists, art historians, curators, and writers. I want to thank Rossella Biscotti, Gregg Bordowitz, María del Carmen Carrión, Margaret Lee, Trevor Paglen and Katy Siegel for their participation in this conversation. The questions and insights that they brought to the table helped to shape the contents here. We are grateful to them and to the other artists, writers, and curators who have contributed to this book. SculptureCenter's curator, Ruba Katrib, has steered this project with care and rigor and I want to thank Lucy Flint for her astute editing.

This book and the *Inquiries into Contemporary Sculpture* series further SculptureCenter's contribution to a broad, international discourse on contemporary art and we are delighted to partner with Black Dog Publishing on this project. Our programs would not be possible without the generous support of our government, foundation, and individual supporters who are named in the colophon of this publication. I want to pay special recognition to our Board of Trustees who support and facilitate the open-ended research and experimentation that has become a hallmark of our program.

Mary Ceruti
Executive Director and Chief Curator

INTRODUCTION
WHAT ABOUT POWER?

Sneaking up behind us, the thing we might "bump into" while looking at a painting, as Barnett Newman famously noted, sculpture always relates to actual space, whether through its presence or even its absence. Tangible or conceptual, big or small, bronze or plastic, sculpture negotiates the physical realm, approaching actuality more than other representational art forms. While increasingly amorphous, sculpture today continues to ask us to think about space, bodies, place, and material. Often enacting these dynamics in forms that embody the "real" rather than the depicted, sculpture is an entity occupying (or not occupying) volume. Through physical presence or the negation of presence, any artwork that touches the broad perimeters of sculpture may engage the politics of portrayal, but cannot avoid the politics of the actualized. From monuments to ritual objects, sculpture requires an embodied and interactive viewer, and as such it engages — perhaps more immediately than other forms of art — social and personal power relations.

The particular power dynamics surrounding sculpture leads us to discussions of architecture, the body, commodity culture, and scale. *What about Power?* considers what forces must be negotiated within the arenas of object making, display, and reception. Do large objects still memorialize, dominate, or intimidate? What energy is contained within small, intimate objects? How do sculptures enter the public sphere, collections, the market? How do they speak to communities, what is their social function? What are the politics of making an object, from sketch to production to presentation? These are a few of the questions we ask about power relations in contemporary sculpture.

The contributors to this volume responded to our question "What about power?" with a range of extended essays, short texts, images, and poems related to their specific interests. "What about power?" in relation to sculpture is an open-ended question that invites many more: How are objects and non-objects — tied to particular sites or circulating in exhibition halls — impacted by dominance and impotence? When do they have power and when do they lose it? Do they endow power? Do they seize power? Do they emphasize or reveal systems of domination? How does sculpture's existence in, or negation of, space affect its power dynamic as distinct from that of, for instance, an image? Power is slippery, even sneaky — it appears and disappears — but it is always there. Tracing the shifty nature of power, the contributors to this book cite examples of when it becomes evident and when it needs to be called out.

Having moved off the pedestal — or choosing to stay on it — sculpture can get as close to enacting the real as any medium. However, even within the space of representation, sculpture has the ability to alter physical and sensorial perceptions. Incorporating the senses that perceive space, including but not limited to vision, sculpture reveals the competing forces of our physical world. Material, immaterial, big, small, interactive, static, and variable in so many other ways, sculpture inspires reimaginings of our habituated travels through space and time.

In preparing this book, we intentionally left the definitions of both sculpture and power loose. We asked each of the contributors to respond to the following statement with an essay, short text, and/or image:

What about Power? looks at the contemporary intersections of power and sculpture. From ritual to monument, sculpture has been embedded within various power dynamics, whether political, spiritual, erotic, or other. Sculpture's relationship to power is distinct from other artistic forms, as it is engaged with particular spatial and physical realms. Hinged on issues around architecture and the body, sculpture reflects on will, subjugation, desire, fetish, and scale. These relationships have shifted throughout time, and we wish to ask where they now stand. What is the power dynamic around sculpture? Does sculpture wield power? If so, what kind? Is it necessary to understand sculpture through power relations? What is the potential of this kind of reading, and what are its pitfalls?

The historians, curators, and artists who have contributed to this volume have their own relationship to the object and to issues of power. Their texts address the role of the monument, what happens to art in the public sphere, the social and political content of objects that circulate through distinct spaces of ritual and contemporary art, and how race and gender are embedded and embodied within sculptural practice. Using sculpture as a starting point, this book speaks to pressing concerns affecting the process of art making and its reception today.

Mary Ceruti and Ruba Katrib

This publication is the second volume in the series *Inquiries into Contemporary Sculpture*, published by Black Dog Publishing, London and SculptureCenter, Long Island City, New York. Posing a sequence of provocative questions, the series offers a vigorous investigation into the meaning and role of sculpture, providing multivalent perspectives rather than definitive answers. This approach is in keeping with SculptureCenter's mission and Black Dog Publishing's interests to push the discourse around sculpture—its production, display, and distribution—into fresh, uncharted, and experimental territories.

Public Image Limited:

On historical allegories of liberty

and their contemporary afterlives

Jörg Heiser

The absence of enthralling imagery in the face of current phenomena of oppression, many of which are invisible and abstract—from digital surveillance to finance—has been lamented for years. For lack of ideas, the media has repeated the same kinds of images over and over: an ethernet plug in front of an NSA emblem; candy-colored pie charts and zigzagging arrows. In the 1980s, the animal rights movement, to put it bluntly, needed images of clubbed seals to gather momentum. The Guy Fawkes mask with its sarcastic smirk, having come to prominence in the wake of the Occupy movement protests, may be an expression of resistance and perseverance.[1] But it cannot replace a visualization of what that struggle actually is against, and for.

What does the absence of such iconic visualization or physical incarnation mean for that stalwart lady, the Statue of Liberty? Turned into cliché by a zillion reproductions on mugs and T-shirts, and mocked by pathological political agendas preventing gun control or promoting blanket mass surveillance, has she become a remnant of a bygone era, a travesty? Travesty or not, it may be urgent now to insist on the values allegorically embodied by that sculptural icon or on the more literal embodiment of these values in the form of the U.S. Constitution.

Jacob Appelbaum is a hacktivist and co-founder of Tor.[2] Being a close associate and supporter of WikiLeaks and an outspoken critic of surveillance practices in the United States, Appelbaum had a number of intimidating encounters with customs and intelligence service personnel that led him to relocate to Berlin, Germany. Whenever he travels across borders, he carries with him a USB stick, anticipating that it will be confiscated as a potential carrier of sensitive data; yet the only thing stored on that stick, in a coded manner, is the U.S. Bill of Rights.[3] It is the perfect gesture to embody the relationship between the invisibility of surveillance, the ungraspability of liberty, and the concrete appeal to the law once decreed to ensure freedom of speech and expression—the First Amendment.

Appelbaum's comment, wrapped in a riddle for over-eager customs officers—a kind of conceptual insistence on the possibility of freedom in the face of its very infringement—reminds me strangely of the opening scene of Franz Kafka's *Amerika* (1911–1914, first published posthumously in 1927). In both cases, a central icon of American liberty is transformed, recoded, to reveal a truth. In Appelbaum's case, it's to expose the dangers of surveillance and the military-industrial complex undermining civil rights; in Kafka's, to expose the violent undercurrent of the civilized-seeming notion of a "land of the free":

> As Karl Rossmann, a poor boy of 16 who had been packed off to America by his
> parents because a servant girl had seduced him and got herself with child by
> him, stood on the liner slowly entering the harbor of New York, a sudden burst
> of sunshine seemed to illumine the Statue of Liberty, so that he saw it in a new
> light, although he had sighted it long before. The arm with the sword rose up as
> if newly stretched aloft, and round the figure blew the free winds of heaven.[4]

With his unmistakable intuitive capability to charge a well-known motif—an immigrant laying eyes on the Statue of Liberty upon entering New York Harbor—with layers of meaning in a manner reminiscent of an intense daydream or ecstatic hallucination, Kafka captures the sublimely contradictory nature of liberty. Rossmann is coming to the U.S. not out of free will, but because he has to; the *seductive* idea of liberty, which he had "sighted long before", is already tangled up with the reality of repudiation by his family ("packed off") as well as by society ("poor", "servant"). But then the clouded sky opens and a sunbeam sheds new light: there it is, the magnificent epiphany, that despite these entanglements, a radically new life might be possible, albeit again amidst danger and

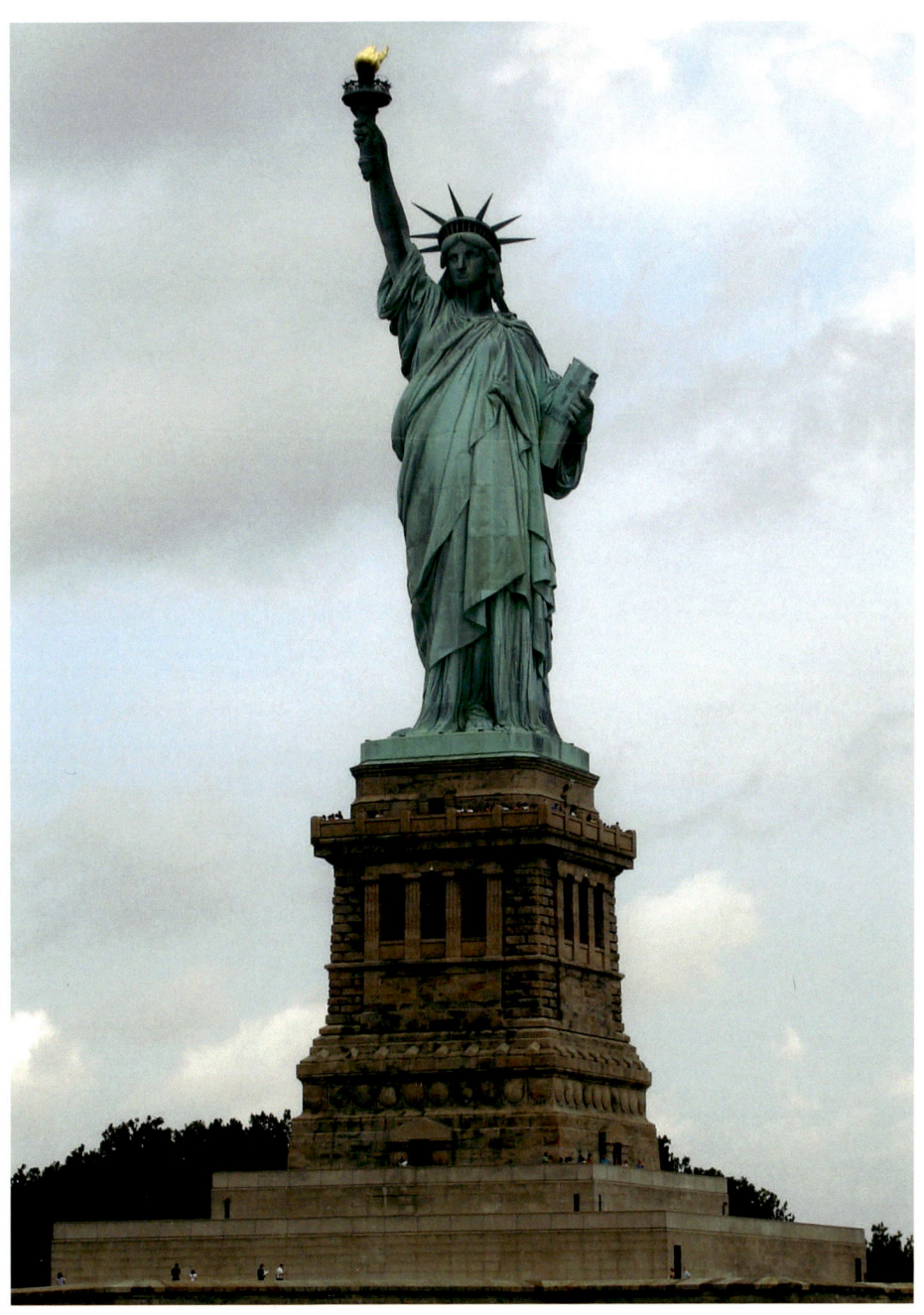

Statue of Liberty, image from public domain.

catastrophe (the sword replacing the homely comfort of the beacon). Liberty, here, is both phallic promise and castrating threat.[5]

Kafka's acute literary sense for the dangers of the individual becoming prey to state apparatuses led him to dark premonitions of the breakdowns of civilization that were still to come. And after they indeed occurred, Hannah Arendt philosophically took stock. Arendt, highly suspicious of romanticism and any idea of mixing up the intimate with the public, would also have avoided—one might have thought—any religious charge of the notion of liberty. In her 1960 lecture "Freedom and Politics", she is careful to distinguish what she calls "political freedom"—meaning "freedom among others"—from the more personal exercise of free will and the rather spiritual experience of inner freedom.[6] But defining the "politically guaranteed public realm" as a precondition for freedom, and warning against any equations of security with political freedom,[7] she goes on to see in the New Testament the idea of an occurrence of the "wholly unexpected", brought about by faith rather than will—the miracle, in the sense of a human action that interrupts "a natural series of events".[8]

Arendt, rather than detecting a religious trait in the idea of political action, delineates the political substance of the religious, at least in terms of Jesus and the New Testament: that the "miracles" performed by humans, just like truly political acts, are new beginnings.[9] In Arendt's view, the biggest combined danger of totalitarian tendencies in politics and of corporate mass culture is that they "stifle initiative and spontaneity as such", that is to say, the faculties that could bring about the unforeseeable, the improbable (one inevitably has to think of state-run as well as corporate data mining, seeking to control and predict behavior, effecting exactly that stifling of spontaneity).[10] Which brings us back to the allegories of liberty. The Statue of Liberty has predecessors: the Roman Republic's founding myth is the death of Lucretia, who killed herself with a dagger after being raped by a tyrant's son, thus inciting an uprising that would lead to the tyrant's overthrow; in postrevolutionary France, it is the allegorical figure of Marianne. Historically, these figures were meant to retroactively represent occurrences of the improbable, the "miracle" of a revolution or declaration of independence. The connection that Arendt makes between the Christian miracle and revolutionary political action could be extended to the modernist avant-garde, who sought to bring the unforeseen, the improbable, into the world.

Statuemania and its discontents

Marcel Duchamp's readymade; the Dadaist/Surrealist fetish object; the geometrically abstracted form in Cubism, Constructivism, and, later, Minimal Art; the incorporation of architecture and performance into the process of creating physical art objects, from Land Art to Actionism to Postminimalism: all of these are ways of making sculpture without sculpture. These innovations negated sculpture in regard to its *sculpted* capacity, that is, the historical understanding of sculpture as shaped or drawn from life (somewhat comparable to the function of 3-D photography/film/print today); drawn from life, but not identical with it—rather, as allegory or carefully molded and wrought naturalist impression, an idea that was still very much central to Auguste Rodin and Medardo Rosso (and, already to a much lesser extent, the young Constantin Brâncuşi).

An obvious reason for the negation of the more traditional notion of sculpture would simply be the saturation of art history, which prompts the desire to progress while responding to the advances of technology and of the natural sciences. Think of the famous anecdote of Duchamp and Brâncuşi, accompanied by Fernand Léger, who in 1912, at the sight of an airplane propeller in a Paris industrial salon, agreed that its elegant abstract shape formed the benchmark of sculpture, of art in general. But maybe the saturation of art history and the rise of machines do not sufficiently explain the move toward negating "traditional" sculpture. Maybe there is another, at least as important, factor that can best be explained by way of a famous Charlie Chaplin film scene and a postcard from Richard Huelsenbeck to fellow Dadaist Tristan Tzara.

The Chaplin scene in question opens *City Lights*, 1931, with the unveiling ceremony for a monument dedicated to "Peace and Prosperity". In front of a crowd of hundreds, a pompous politician and a frumpy donor offer remarks; we don't hear what they say, but their voices are presented—in this late silent movie competing with talkies—by nervous Kazoo wheezing that mocks their empty phrases, anticipating Chaplin's Hitler gibberish in *The Great Dictator*, 1940. The cloth is finally lifted off the monument to reveal a sleeping tramp (Chaplin) curled up on a statue's lap as if on a too-small sofa. The statue is one of three allegorical figures in antique attire: the seated female is accompanied by two males, one of whom, reclining, wields a sword, while the other, kneeling, holds up a hand in a gesture of warding off. The stiff bathos of the constellation—reminiscent of a Sophocles tableau in a school play—is sharply contrasted by the tramp, who, still half-asleep, casually scratches his head and knee, to the indignation of the notables gathered. Finally awake and aware of his situation, he courteously lifts his hat and tries to get away, but the seat of his pants gets caught on the sword. A policeman in parade uniform barks at him to get off, but as the national anthem resounds, the cop has to snap to attention and salute; the tramp also tries to brace solemnly, but as he can't get his feet fully on the ground, he pedals like a hamster in a wheel, followed by further mishaps excessively extending the embarrassment, from sitting on the swordsman's face to his nose touching the open hand of the other male statue, effectively thumbing it at the proceedings. The implicit comment is that the monument, despite its appellation of "Peace and Prosperity", was not erected for the sake of people like this homeless tramp—people excluded from prosperity, and thus, the benefits of peace. It was erected to celebrate the powers that be. But here, by merely and gently *sleeping*, then scratching, pedalling, and so forth, the tramp deflates that power, if only for a moment. A sudden, comic beam of truth.

Huelsenbeck's postcard to Tzara symbolically shrank another monument, the 91-meter-high Monument to the Battle of the Nations, a Wilhelmine structure made of dark granite on concrete that was erected in 1913 in Leipzig, Germany, to commemorate Napoleon's defeat there a hundred years earlier. Across the image of this exaltation of the Germanic national spirit Huelsenbeck had written "MERDE". However this deflation of the monument, crossed out with a virtually screamed "Shit!", was a personalized message between friends and fellow artists—mild flatulence in comparison to the monstrosity of the towering monument that itself looks like a scatological remnant, a phallic turd shat by the God of War as he strode through on his way to the trenches of Verdun, immune to the blood shed by millions. *MERDE* indeed.

Chaplin's silent dream and Huelsenbeck's silent scream both indicate a profound discontent with the outcome of almost a century of "statuemania".[11] After the upheavals of the Napoleon Wars, Europe became increasingly littered with monuments celebrating kings and queens, generals and war heroes, and, not least, female state allegories: Britannia, Germania, and France's Marianne. Meant to represent pride and sovereignty, these statues bespeak an anxiety that underlay the attempt to corral people into mythological national wholes in order to ward off their taking too literally any promises of equality and freedom in the wake of the various crises, coups, and revolutions that had borne the nations in question. Societies were newly and increasingly fractured by industrialization and individualization, the amassing of extreme wealth and the spread of mass poverty, and by capitalist prosperity paired with colonialist ruthlessness—by what Karl Marx simply called "contradictions".

In the face of these contradictions, what these statues offered was a phantasmatic unity, wholeness, against an outer or inner enemy. But the sheer number and increasing ugliness of all these monuments came back to haunt the cities, exposing the warding-off anxiety in an embarrassing way—at least in the eyes of artists and political activists eager to recall unfulfilled dreams of liberation.

Many of these statues turned into travesty the female allegories of freedom that had their roots in antiquity, early Christianity, the Renaissance, and the French Revolution.[12] For those who joined the Constructivist and Dadaist avant-gardes, the very idea of an allegorical figure—even of "figure" as such—had become kitsch. Hence, for many artists it was impossible to propose these allegories without feeling utterly ridiculous (a sentiment still prominent today among artists and architects), and the task became to radically abolish such an aesthetic and replace it with something new. Vasily Kandinsky wanted to rescue spirituality from figurative sentimentality. Kazimir Malevich started his 1915 Suprematist manifesto by saying that "Only with the disappearance of a habit of mind which sees in pictures little corners of nature, Madonnas and shameless Venuses, *shall we witness a work of pure, living art.*"[13] And when Vladimir Tatlin first presented the model of his *Monument to the Third International* in 1920—a double helix meant to represent Hegel's philosophical concept of dialectics—Vladimir Mayakovsky remarked that it was the first Russian monument "without a beard", slyly alluding to an aesthetic continuum between statues of the Tsars and those of Marx/Engels and Lenin.[14] While female allegories of freedom weren't really that present in Tsarist or Bolshevik Russia either, by the time the colossal figure *The Motherland Calls*, rivaled in size only by the Statue of Liberty, was unveiled in 1967 in Volgograd (the former Stalingrad), it was clear whom this allegory was meant to stand for: the millions of Soviet soldiers who had lost their lives fighting back Hitler's Wehrmacht. But any assumption of that allegory also being a representation of individual liberties—citizen rights and so forth—was clearly out of the question. *The Motherland Calls* is a dynamic female figure holding up a huge sword, as if striding into battle, her mouth wide open as she calls to arms the invisible troops behind her. She represents not liberty, but subordination to the cause of war. Constructivism had been cleansed from Soviet official aesthetics, and even though the Stalinist era was over, it remained terminally replaced by socialist realism—which was, strictly speaking, not realist but idealist, depicting not how things were, but how, allegorically and ideologically, they should be. Just months after the inauguration of *The Motherland Calls*, the Prague Spring was crushed by Soviet tanks.

Had there ever been, in contrast, a convincing *abstract* memorial to liberty? After Tatlin's audacious unrealized plan (as unrealized as the idealized promises of revolutionary communism), what comes to mind is Ludwig Mies van der Rohe's Revolutionary Monument to Rosa Luxemburg and Karl Liebknecht, erected in Berlin in 1926. In the wake of the eventually unsuccessful socialist uprising in the city in January 1919, Luxemburg and Liebknecht had been murdered by right-wing paramilitaries (apparently with the tacit approval of leading Social Democrats in government).[15] Mies was not a Socialist, or even overtly political; he opportunistically joined the Reichskulturkammer in 1934, which did not prevent the Nazis from eradicating his monument around that time. But even if they did so solely to eliminate a site of gathering and commemoration for Socialists, Mies's design certainly was up against Nazi aesthetics as well. A brick structure of rectangular beams or platforms horizontally stacked on top of one another in an elegantly irregular way, it did not present idealized allegorical figures of leaders, heroes, or martyrs. Instead, it offered a geometrically reduced suggestion—or allegory?—of society as layers of interaction, emphasizing horizontal planes over vertical hierarchies, not forced into a strict order but given room to move sideways (even if he was a political opportunist, Mies seemed to understand the ideals of Socialism better than many of its proponents). The question is whether Mies approved of the metal star with hammer and sickle mounted to one side of the structure like a badge of honor pinned to a proud hero's chest—it feels more like a compromise. In any case, Mies' memorial offered the idea of a site for commemorating important and courageous individuals that, however, purposefully stopped short of turning them into icons, emphasizing their contribution in terms of bigger ideas and wider collectives. Yet, despite all these qualities Mies' Revolutionary Memorial did not become a blueprint for a new kind of enthralling aesthetics that prompts a vision of liberty (or struggle for liberty, as personified by a figure such as Luxemburg). It just didn't offer any point of entry for empathy or identification, and was instead a consciously brutal, rough structure—after all, though called a "revolutionary memorial", it was a de facto mausoleum. The early Modernist program of replacing the exhausted mystery of allegorical statues with the bold clarity of grand-scale abstract forms, from Tatlin to Mies, has not prevailed—at least not in regard to representations of liberty. There is one register, however, in which geometric abstraction *has* prevailed: as representation of trauma and civilizational breakdown, from Viktor Tolkin's *Monument to Struggle and Martyrdom*,1969, at the Majdanek concentration camp near Lublin, Poland, to Peter Eisenman's *Memorial to the Murdered Jews of Europe*, 2005, in Berlin.

Now: The return of the allegoric sculpture of liberty as copy
Just as nineteenth-century academic statue making has become a cliché, so has the avant-garde promise of creating the improbable. One way to act on this development has been to document, appropriate, and re-enact the last avant-gardes: to reconsider and restage past achievements, find cracks in the genius demeanor, pay homage through parody. Thus, even that tired claim of "questioning perception" is deflated and yet, at the same time, resuscitated: we thought we knew this history, this aesthetics, this work, but did we?

In his series *Organized Décor [Improved Partisan Monuments]*, begun in 2001, Austrian artist Marko Lulić has appropriated the largely abstract designs of Yugoslavian monuments commissioned by the State (mostly during the 1960s and 70s under Tito), shrinking them to decorative domestic size. Lulić's repurposed solemn monuments to martyrs of the struggle for liberation from oppressors also include versions of Mies' aforementioned memorial, adopted in several finishes, including plexiglass, chipboard, and aluminum, minus the flagstaff and the hammer and sickle, and reduced to roughly the size of a little van (the original monument was more like a small house). The title *Entertainment Center Mies*, 2003–2004, again suggests the purposeful formalist emptying out of the original design, while the gesture exposes, deliberately and glaringly, that very process in modernism at large: the way that designs once meant to thrust forward into a utopian future have gradually become shrunk and shriveled objects for nostalgia; and how forms that were meant to be inherently progressive, serious, and antihierarchic—the horizontal beams, held in dynamic balance, of Mies' memorial—are, of course, not immune to being exploited for "entertainment center" business ends. If doubts remain about how much Lulić is in on the parody and how much he perpetuates what he criticizes, these are doubts that the artist himself cultivates by returning to the subject and testing other repurposing transformations: in performance pieces of recent years, for example, he revisits the sculptures in brief phrases of dance choreography. Ultimately, Lulić's argument is that temporary props, fleeting re-enactments, and frivolous parodies are more appropriate to the painful labor of commemoration than any construction occupying a big space for a long time could ever be.

In her video essay *Turbo Sculpture*, 2011–2013, Berlin-based artist Aleksandra Domanović explores the dramatic lack of a progressive idea of history and the future in the Balkans, a region stuck in incessant war-traumatized mythologizing. The artist, who was born in Novi Sad (Serbia), considers a phenomenon that has sprung up across ex-Yugoslavian states in the wake of the Western Balkan wars of the 1990s: impromptu figurative public sculptures, erected in the center of towns, that are dedicated to Hollywood actors such as Bruce Lee and Johnny Depp, and even fictional characters, like Rocky Balboa or Batman. Domanović traces a genealogy that leads back to the clever, monstrously effective concept of "Turbo Folk", a local musical genre marrying techno beats with Balkan folklore melodies. The resulting blend is one of raunchy, boozy partying and chauvinist thug sentimentality. "Turbo" has become a prefix that denotes the post-1989 turmoil of rapid transition from socialism to neo-liberal capitalism, unregulated amid vacuums and abuses of power and wealth. *Turbo Sculpture* can be read as the symptom of a post-traumatic unwillingness to look back at the darkest moments of the 1990s Balkan wars—memorials against memory. With the divisions between the war parties remaining largely unchanged, and war crimes still being considered heroic acts by some—with no coming to terms and consolation in sight—the only solution is to fill the gap with an externalized fantasy, using the popular denominators that the U.S.-led, globalized entertainment industry offers. When a life-size bronze statue of a bare-chested Bruce Lee assuming a fighting pose, with nunchuks, was erected in the center of Mostar, Herzegovina, in 2005, the youth group and collective Urban Movement, who had initiated the project, were careful to point out that Lee was chosen as a heroic figure because he was "far enough away from us so that nobody can ask what he did during World War II" and represented "part of our idea of justice: good guys can win". In a city riven by the post-Yugoslav ethnic secessions among the Croats, Serbs, and Bosniaks, "the Chinese-American martial arts actor represented a bridging of cultures, an emblem of the fight against ethnic divisions", according to the matter-of-fact voiceover in Domanović's video. But doubts remain whether the optimistic calculation actually adds up: whether fictional characters serving as sculptural substitutes actually have an integrating, consoling effect. Even if the Bruce Lee statue hadn't within months been vandalized innumerable times and finally taken down, the question is whether the inability to single out real-life role models—or real-life traumas—as somehow emblematically representative of the community, rather than fictional or "exotic" ones external to it, isn't ultimately an expression of more than just the inability to agree on such an "internal" role model. Rather, that inability seems an expression of the very inexistence of a proper community in the first place.

Domanović's piece translates the inflation of monuments—Tarzan, King Arthur, Batman, and Madonna are at the planning stage—into a peculiar editing principle. Throughout, still images appear atop one another in different formats, centered symmetrically, so that with the next image the fringes of the previous ones remain visible, like decals of different sizes stuck on top of one another. While this digital effect, mimicking a physical quality, would be considered tacky and inappropriate in professional film editing, here it seems to congenially correspond to the subject matter: history is written by way of erasure, as one layer of imagery overrides the previous one. But the past still shows through at the seams.

Rather than the likeness of a current celebrity, the Statue of Liberty is an allegory for an age-old idea. Still, for many it has long been a farce. So what does the Statue still stand for? Maybe a hint comes courtesy of an almost excessively ambitious sculptural project that Vietnamese-Danish artist Danh Vo embarked on in 2011. *We The People*, 2011–2014, is a 1:1 rendition of the Statue broken down into 250 individual parts made of thin copper sheets, not yet covered with verdigris. If they were assembled onto a skeleton construction, as in the case of the original, they would form an exact replica. Instead, the individual fragments, which were produced over the course of three years in a specialized coppersmith's shop in China, have been shipped around the world to various exhibitions to be displayed *as* fragments, sometimes giving a clear hint of the figure they belong to (a toe or an eye), sometimes remaining an abstract fold or knob. The artist is adamant that the installation crew, rather than he or a curator, determine how exactly each individual piece is installed. At times remaining on wooden pallets, at times put directly onto the floor or leaned against the wall, the pieces remain in a limbo halfway between transport, storage, and exhibition.

What does it mean to make a full-scale replica of such a gargantuan statue, and—literally—break down the components? First of all, the production process itself is problematic. "I didn't like the fact that [the copper sheets] had to be made in China—because it adds a layer of meaning to the piece", Vo has stated. "This is obviously related to how IKEA and a lot of other companies outsource work to cheaper places.... I think the decision was due to the fact that they were able to make it. In the West this technique is only used for mending sculptures."[16] The pitfalls of globalization that can be read into the piece's production are not, however, Vo's main concern here: "If I had a wish, I would make that dimension disappear." The decision to let the installation crew decide the exact placement of the objects also serves this wish to avoid overdetermination—or, to be more precise, it shifts the emphasis to concerns of practicality and collectivity. Once you stand in front of one of the fragments, any remaining assumption of sculptural aura as well as of aesthetically determined installation evaporate. Instead, you are confronted with an abstracted detail of an allegory of liberty left in some more-or-less random place, all dressed up and nowhere to go. You feel prompted to examine the fragments as if they were forensic evidence. As shattered as the Statue is the idea of a united "we" of beholders. Which brings the title of the piece into play: *We The People*, the famous opening phrase of the Preamble to the United States Constitution. In relation to the fragmented nature of the piece, the title begs the questions, Who is that "we", and who are "the people"? Who is speaking, and in whose name? The proud confidence the phrase may once have had is battered by hot and cold wars, increasing inequality, and the techno-narcissist disassociations of contemporary mass culture. An image by Vo announcing a Public Art Fund installation of a number of the fragments in New York's City Hall Park and Brooklyn Bridge Park in the summer of 2014 brings forth an acerbic diagnosis of liberty's current currency: a rendering of the Statue of Liberty as an abstract computer drawing in black lines on gray with numbered parts, some of which are highlighted in red, as in a butcher's beef chart. Fragments of a once-proud whole are either scavenged and sold off into eager collectors' hands, lost in the landscape like ruins of antiquity, or, like the Statue of Liberty in the closing scene of *Planet of the Apes*, 1968, half-sunk into beach sand. If Vo wanted to avoid adding meaning, in this instance he successfully failed: as the "politically guaranteed public realm" that Arendt described as a precondition of freedom becomes eroded by overreaching state security and surveillance concerns as well as corporate investment interests, the great ideal of Liberty is chopped and sold in pieces. Does that *suspend* the idea of liberty as represented by an allegorical statue or a written constitution? No, because as long as it's an *idea* rather than an entirely forgotten, ancient state of mind, it can be rediscovered, reactivated against those who have sold or suffocated it.

There may still be situations and places where "mere" visual representations of allegories of liberty gain some currency. But maybe the time is also ripe for "postrepresentational", coded, or performative languages of form that bring concepts of copying and recirculation of earlier figurative sculptures and icons to a broader public. There are forms of protest that

(overleaf) Danh Vo, *We The People* (detail), 2011–2014. Copper. Collection François Odermatt, Montreal. Presented by Public Art Fund at Brooklyn Bridge Park and City Hall Park, 17 May–5 December 2014. Photo: James Ewing, Courtesy Public Art Fund, NY.

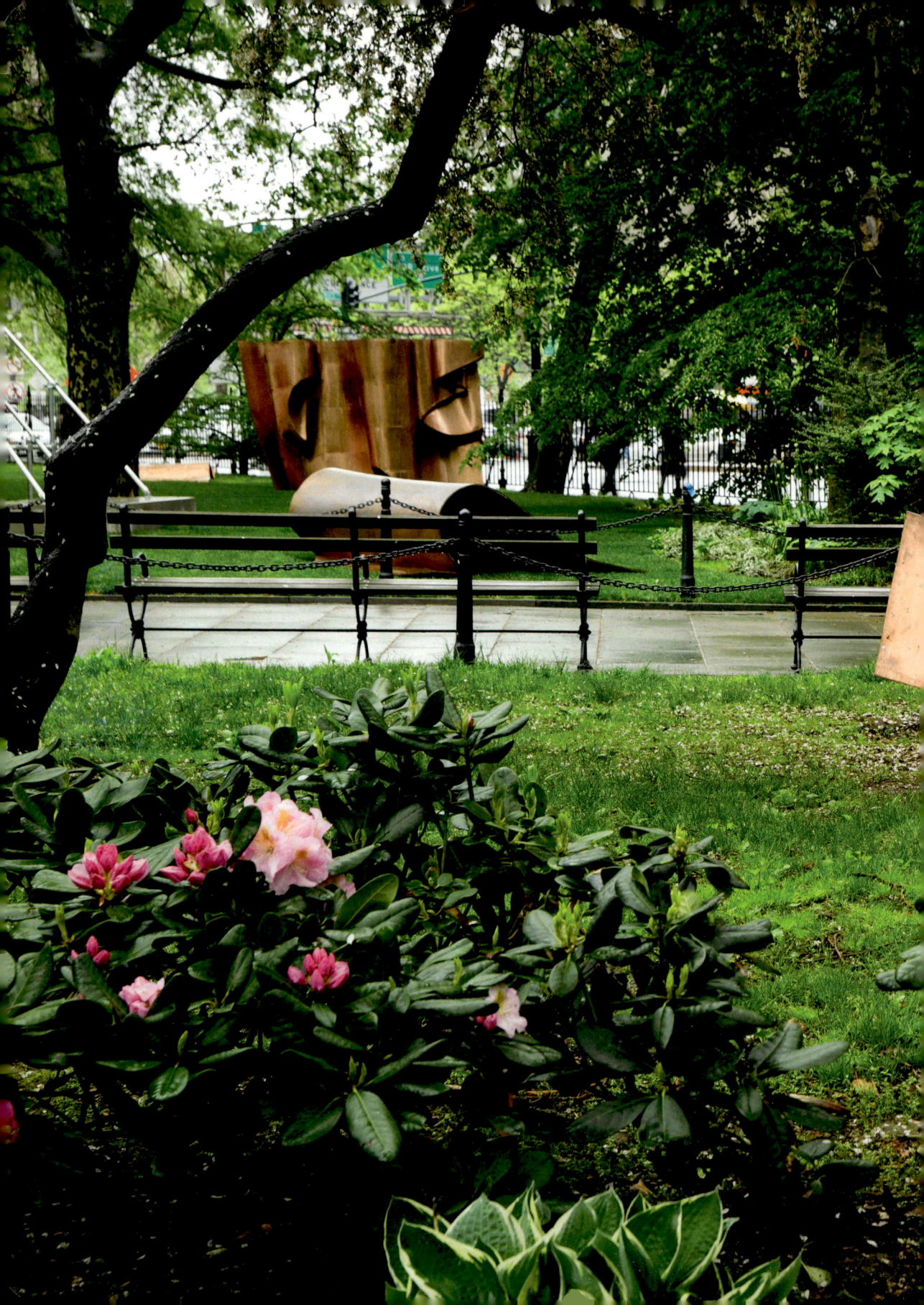

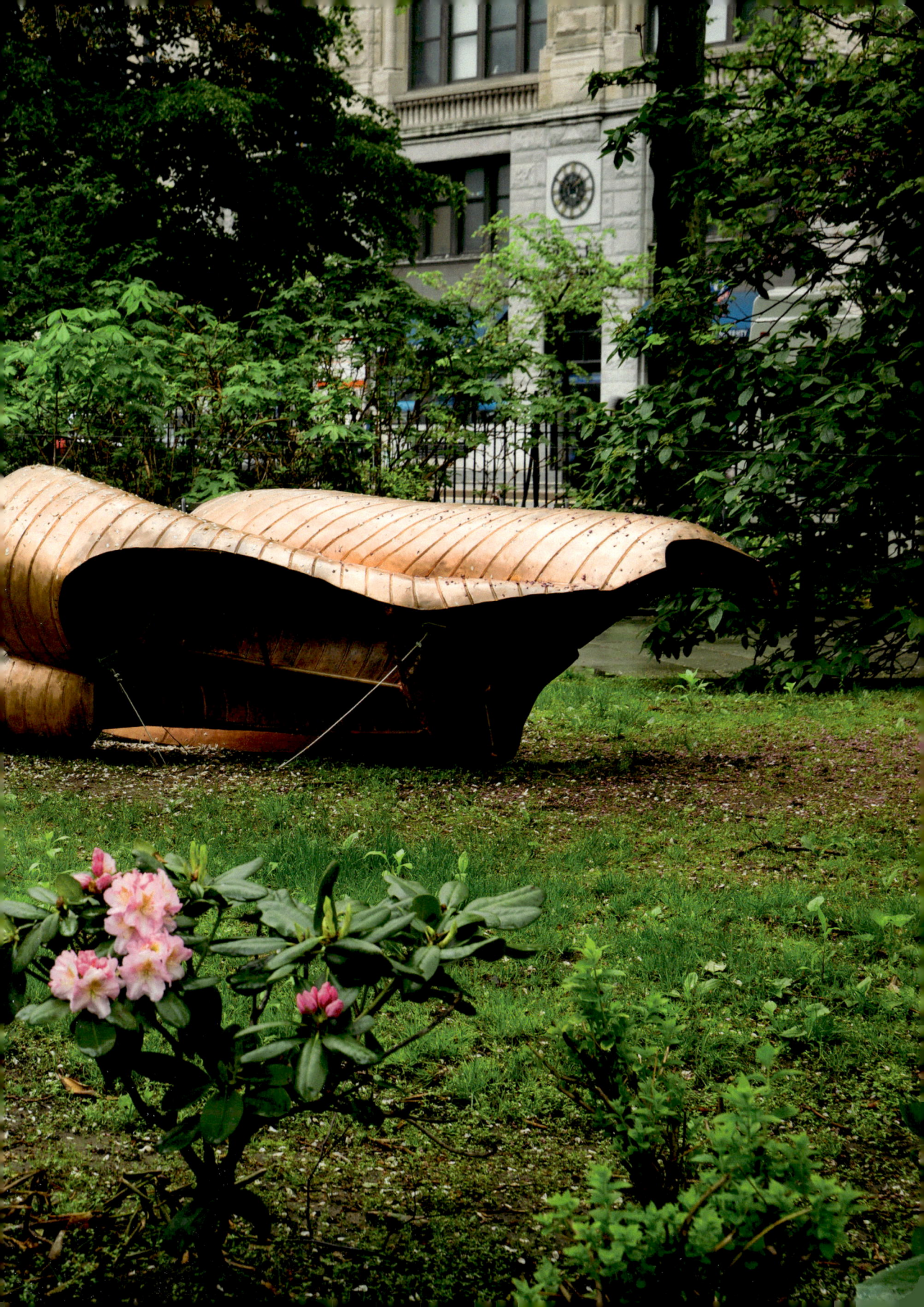

seem to do well without allegories of liberty, not least because they become an allegory of the struggle for liberty in their own right. After demonstrators in Istanbul's Gezi Park were violently evicted in June 2013, the choreographer Erdem Gündüz stood silently, for hours on end, staring at the flags outside Atatürk Culture Center on nearby Taksim Square. The concept went viral under the hashtag #standingman (#durunadam in Turkish), prompting thousands to follow Gündüz' example. There is no heroic pose or gesture, no iconic silhouette or striking slogan — just people standing around, images that by definition cannot be as enthralling as the verbal description of the action or the action itself. That is, doing something ordinary — pausing, standing — but simply for too long for it to be without intention.

In order to be able to go out in public and, like Gündüz, do the "impossible", you first need — to follow Hannah Arendt's line of thought — an intimate sphere for the experience of successful collectivity, where you can start to think and question, to generate innovative and spontaneous ideas, to muster the courage to eventually go out and act. That is the trouble we're in: that intimate sphere is under attack, with our digital selves under surveillance or lured to give away our thoughts "for free", to be mined in the big data stream. The (re)establishment of credible public representations of liberty, whether allegorical or "real", is preconditioned by the reestablishment of privacy. To achieve that goal, juridical, technological, and political measures, as well as continuing protest, will be needed to rein in ruthless data collectors of all kinds. Public sculpture — whether abstract or figurative, whether as an allegory set in stone or performed and copied — should be a part of that struggle.

1   The Guy Fawkes mask is based on illustrator David Lloyd's design for Alan Moore's dystopic graphic novel *V for Vendetta*, 1992, turned into the eponymous 2006 movie and eventually adopted by protesters associated with the website 4chan and the hacktivist network Anonymous.
2   Tor is a software/network designed to allow you to surf the Internet undetected, initially developed to help dissidents in different parts of the world to communicate unintercepted, and funded as such by numerous government bodies.
3   See the ABC News website at tinyurl.com/AppelbaumBillofRights, accessed 30 June 2014.
4   Kafka, Franz, *Amerika*, trans. Willa and Edwin Muir, London: Vintage Books, 2005, p. 12.
5   Notably, in the original Kafka does not use the common German translation of "Statue of Liberty", "*Freiheitsstatue*", but "*Statue der Freiheitsgöttin*", which translates as "Statue of the Goddess of Liberty". "*Freiheitsgöttin*" in German alliterates with the more common "*Fruchtbarkeitsgöttin*", "Goddess of Fertility" — a connotation that again ties in with the theme of an illegitimate child, and of a pagan rather than enlightened view of life.
6   Arendt, Hannah, "Freedom and Politics: A Lecture", *Chicago Review* 14, no. 1, spring 1960, p. 29.
7   Arendt, "Freedom and Politics", pp. 31–32.
8   Arendt, "Freedom and Politics", p. 43.
9   Note the similarity of Arendt's concept of the true political event to Alain Badiou's.
10 Arendt, "Freedom and Politics", p. 45.
11 The notion of "statuemania", in French "*statuomanie*", was arguably first thoroughly discussed by Maurice Aghulon in "La 'Statuomanie' et l'histoire", *Ethnologie française* 8, nos. 2–3, 1978, pp. 145–173.
12 The question of why, historically, allegories of liberty have, almost exclusively, been female, remains to be explored in depth, though two points can be mentioned here in brief. The obvious reason would be that, grammatically, in Latin and Greek (as well as French and German), the word "freedom" is feminine. That said, from a patriarchal, male perspective, the concept of the allegory calls on the Other (the woman, the goddess) as representation of an abstract, universal idea (freedom, equality, independence), even though incarnations of that very Other are excluded from the ideal. Freedom is associated with the wild Other until freedom is actually achieved. See Warner, Marina, *Monuments and Maidens: The Allegory of Female Form*, New York: Atheneum, 1985.
13 Malevich, Kazimir, "From Cubism and Futurism to Suprematism: The New Realism in Painting", 1915–1916, in Charles Harrison and Paul Wood, eds., *Art in Theory 1900–1990: An Anthology of Changing Ideas*, London: Blackwell Publishing, 1992, p. 173.
14 Quoted in Dillon, Brian, "The Poetry of Metal", *The Guardian*, 25 July 2009 tinyurl.com/TatlinBeard, accessed 6 September 2014.
15 See Gietinger, Klaus, *Der Konterrevolutionär / Waldemar Pabst — eine deutsche Karriere*, Hamburg: Edition Nautilus, 2008, p. 394.
16 Danh Vo, in the video "Danh Vo–We The People", produced by the Statens Museum for Kunst, Copenhagen, tinyurl.com/DanhVoWeThePeople, accessed 30 June 2014.

To See and Then to Burn

Candice Hopkins

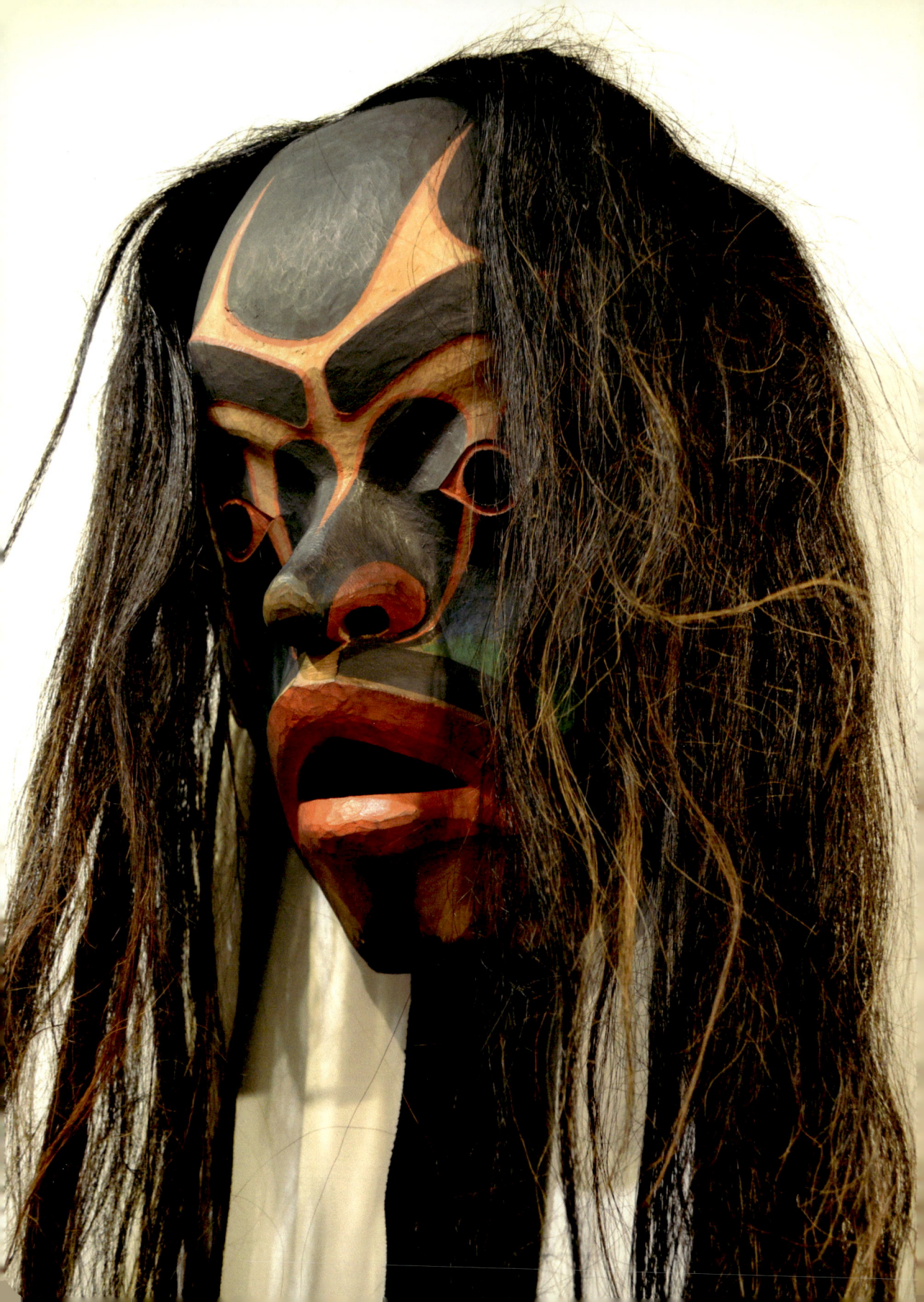

The sacred masks were treated like divinities themselves.[1]
– Claude Lévi-Strauss

I remember the first time I saw one of Beau Dick's masks. The mask was large. Too large to wear, made instead to hang on a gallery wall. Carved wood so dark it appeared charred. The face was both male and female. Long, coarse black hair fell to either side, mixing with the figure's mustache, which curled over red lips fixed in a permanent O as though howling. I stood transfixed by this object, which seemed to hover at the threshold between the nameable and the unnameable. As Jean-Luc Nancy observes: "The fetish is in fact the artifice *par excellence* or *par essence*" (the word *fetish* deriving from the Portuguese *feitifo*, "artificial").[2] The mask was a fetish, yet it refused my fetishization, emerging instead from the context of ritual as an object of disguise, transformation, and metamorphosis. Its artifice is what lent it life. "The fetish is the *being-there* of a desire, an expectation, an imminence, a power and its presentiment, a force interred in the form and exhumed by it."[3] It was the being-there of desire that held my gaze. Is an object's material nature a source of its power, or does that power reside somewhere else? Can an object disrupt the power relations that are set into motion the moment that it is placed in a gallery or museum? Can it disrupt the (still-prevalent) impulse to attach the word "primitive" to this object despite increasingly broad definitions of artistic practice?

In the summer of 2012, Dick performed something of a power transposition. It began with a solo exhibition at a Vancouver gallery that presented a series of carved masks and sculptures. Midway through the show's run, 40 masks were removed and taken to an island off the coast of British Columbia, to the small settlement of Alert Bay, where they were ceremonially burned. The artist invited his community, as well as artists, curators, and gallerists, to Alert Bay to witness the act. For Dick, the burning was not an end but a beginning, the masks' destruction part of a larger cycle bound with the obligation that accompanies tradition and the strict protocols of ritual. As the artist explained about the objects following the burning: "What we have to do is recreate them—and that keeps them alive."[4]

At a time when power is more deeply tied to money than ever before, Dick's project was a means to short-circuit the commodification of Northwest Coast ceremonial objects, preventing them from becoming fetishes in the service not of ritual but of capital. For the artist, ensuring that these objects are used as intended "takes away any monetary value they have in this world and makes [them] real".[5] Destruction becomes an active part of creation by detaching objects from a confining system. With his gesture, Dick has gotten at something: at the moment that an object becomes a commodity, its true nature dissipates, sliding like ashes between spread fingers. The source of resistance is the desire to be real. In Indigenous Northwest Coast societies, the most valuable objects cannot be owned. Passed down through generations, these ceremonial objects are hidden away in decorated boxes for safekeeping when they are not in use. The masks exist in the cyclical time of ritual. Ceremony ruptures the division between the historical and the contemporary—these objects thread their way through time, being continually remade in the same manner irrespective of changes around them.

Mask burning forms part of a potlatch ceremony that remains central to the Kwakwa̱ka̱'wakw people of Alert Bay. Perceived as a threat to Western economic interests, in the late 1800s potlatching was banned in both Canada and the United States. In a potlatch, status is

Beau Dick, *The Boy Who Fell From Heaven*, 2012.
Photo: Naza Del Rosal Ortiz, Courtesy Fazakas Gallery.

gained by the wealth you give away rather than by the goods you accumulate. Originally, the host would distribute, or gift, so much wealth that he was left ostensibly bankrupt (though, according to the social contract, he would be repaid later with interest). Described as a "worse than useless custom" by Indian agents acting on behalf of the government, the ceremony was regarded as "wasteful, unproductive, and contrary to 'civilized' values".[6] When the custom didn't come to a halt altogether, participants were jailed or charged heavy fines. Forced underground, the practice was performed in secret.[7]

The U.S. did not drop the ban until 1934, and Canada followed suit only in 1951. Beau Dick's performance clarified that his masks have an exchange value that is not based on currency but on social agreement. The potlatch and the objects created for it have found their way into modern art and theory: the ceremony inspired the Situationists to name their periodical *Potlatch*; its creative destruction moved Georges Bataille and Marcel Mauss to author books on the subject (*The Accursed Share* and *The Gift*, respectively); the objects' abstraction influenced Marcel Duchamp; and their connection to the subconscious was significant to the surrealists, particularly André Breton.

Potlatch objects were first exhibited in 1927 at the National Gallery of Canada in Ottawa. *Exhibition of Canadian West Coast Art: Native and Modern* attempted to do two things: first, posit objects made by indigenous peoples as art and not ethnography; second, make the case for the emergence of a new and distinctly Canadian painting style that borrowed liberally from Native aesthetic practices. Valued for their affinity with modern art, traditional objects had always been proximate to art, but were not considered art in and of themselves; they are now often regarded as creative production contemporaneous with art, but, again, not as contemporary art. As Dick is well aware, such objects expose the limitations of an art world that aspires to be global, as well as the inability of art discourse to fully account for objects as complex as these masks.

In the announcement sent out in advance of the exhibition, the gallery provided some context to the event:

> This series of masks and ritual knowledge are owned by Beau's family, passed down from generation to generation. They are made roughly, and are worn in a dancing series for four years only, then burned. This grouping is nearing the end of its cycle, and midway through the exhibition the 40 *Atlakim* masks will be taken to Alert Bay to be danced one final time at a Potlatch, and then destroyed. A new set will be carved only to go through the same cycle, and so on.[8]

In a potlatch, the role of witness carries great responsibility:

> The Kwakwạkạ'wakw have always been extremely industrious and they soon began to use the European economic system to reinforce and expand the potlatch, buying items that were given away to the 'witnesses' in attendance at potlatches as payment for remembering and recording the events that take place during the potlatch. This is an extremely important aspect of the potlatch as it is the means of recording the history of the Kwakwạkạ'wakw.[9]

Dick has accorded this role to his audience, guests to his community. It is now their duty to remember and to record. With the market for contemporary art so inflated, it serves us well to remember other values attached to objects. Arjun Appadurai reminds us in *The Social Life of Things* that "even though from a *theoretical* point of view human actors encode things with significance, from a *methodological* point of view it is the things-in-motion that illuminate their human and social context."[10] Beau Dick has mobilized another value system. His action is a reminder of the power that still rests in tradition and custom, and the influence and meaning that is held in objects that circulate within these other systems.

1   Lévi-Strauss, Claude, and Yves Cantraine, "North American Masks", in *TDR: The Drama Review* 26 (4), winter 1982, p. 5.
2   Nancy, Jean-Luc, and Thomas C. Platt, "The Two Secrets of the Fetish", in *Diacritics* 31 (2), summer 2001, p. 4.
3   Nancy and Platt, "The Two Secrets of the Fetish", p. 6.
4   Dawkins, A.B.C., "Beau Dick Burning His Masks", in *Alphabet Review* online, 15 August 2012, thealphabetreview.blogspot.com/2012/08/beau-dick-burning-his-masks.html, accessed 6 May 2014.
5   Dawkins, "Beau Dick Burning His Masks".
6   Sprout, G.M., quoted in Douglas Cole and Ira Chaikin, *An Iron Hand upon the People: The Law against the Potlatch on the Northwest Coast*, Vancouver: Douglas and McIntyre, 1990, p. 15.
7   Potlatches were sometimes scheduled specifically during stormy weather when the authorities did not like to travel. Potlatching practices also became disjointed at times; gifts were handed out separately from when the dancing took place or they were disguised as holiday presents or charity". Unsigned text, "On the Suppression of the Potlatch", U'Mista Cultural Centre website, umista.org/masks_story/en/ht/potlatch02.html, accessed 10 May 2014.
8   Quoted in a press release for the exhibition on the Macaulay Fine Art website, mfineart.ca/exhibitions/past/beau-dick-exhibition-2012, accessed 24 June 2014.
9   Quoted on the U'Mista Cultural Centre website.
10 Appadurai, Arjun, ed., *The Social Life of Things: Commodities in Cultural Perspective*, Cambridge, U.K.: Cambridge University Press, 1986, p. 5.

The Fable of the Slave
and the Sphinx

Malik Gaines

This struggle may be a moral one: or it may be a physical one: or it may be both moral and physical: but it must be a struggle. Power concedes nothing without a demand.
– Frederick Douglass

The quote from Douglass' speech "West Indian Emancipation", delivered in 1857 in Canandaigua, New York, goes on: "It never did and it never will." The section excerpted above appears on a flyer distributed in 2011 by an Indianapolis advocacy group, Citizens Against Slave Image (CASI), which protested plans for a privately commissioned public sculpture by the artist Fred Wilson titled *E Pluribus Unum*. The flyer is styled to resemble a nineteenth-century announcement, seemingly alluding to posters that, historically, advertised runaway slaves, or promoted abolitionist causes, or engaged in that particular drama in one way or another. The weathered paper background and old-timey typeface coexist in careful ambivalence with the informational Web address posted at the bottom of the page, part of which reads "1slave_enough." The design tactic indicates a knowing understanding of the ways historical appropriation may shape and frame contemporary politics, though the campaign promoted by the flyer expressed no patience with this tactic as a context for Wilson's proposed meta-monument. I mention this project sometimes in my role as a teacher, when I come across students and colleagues who find themselves frustrated and befuddled by the ways blackness refuses to satisfactorily resolve itself within the realm of representation by producing an ethical, agreeable, and incontestably efficacious image or form. These days, to those students and colleagues, I find myself saying something like, "It never did and it never will."

Wilson's proposed work was a two-story-high representation of a nineteenth-century figure repositioned to make a critically powerful and aesthetically moving public statement. The proposal was widely discussed in the Indianapolis media and covered nationally as arts news. The artist gave several interviews during the process and delivered a talk on the matter in 2011 at the New School in New York, presented by the Public Art Fund, which is where I became aware of the proposal. He explained that in researching the monuments of Indianapolis, a city littered with them, he had discovered only one African American representation. This figure is situated in a scene at the base of the Soldiers and Sailors Monument, a 285-foot-high neoclassical tower protruding from the historic center of civic life in the city, designed by a German architect and constructed between 1888 and 1901, and depicting numerous bodies in historic action. This figure is masculine, black, shirtless, and attractively muscular. He is seated with his right arm outstretched, holding a broken chain. He is positioned against a gigantic female figure's shield, steadied in her left hand, which declares *E Pluribus Unum*. Elaborately draped, the woman hoists an American flag, and presumably represents Victory or Liberty, or some such personification, some great *Unum*. She occupies the center of a scene that begins on the fully articulated plinth on which she stands and recedes into a pictorial frieze behind her, where soldiers and other figures strike dynamic war-related poses. In front of this scenario, the African American man, evidently a freed slave, sits with his right foot dangling over the edge of the plinth, alongside a sheaf of beautifully detailed grains. He is up front and low. His gaze is focused upward toward the lady spirit of power, whose own gaze is directed outward toward eternity.

Though this scene is prominently central, around it are others rendered in stone and metal, at shifting scales, stretching down into a circular plaza of fountains, pools, steps, lawns, and gorgeous lanterns, and up toward an obelisk-like tower, on top of which, hundreds of feet above, another womanly fantasy poses with a sword and torch. Since 1962, this entire structure has been transformed annually into a simulated Christmas tree lit by a conical

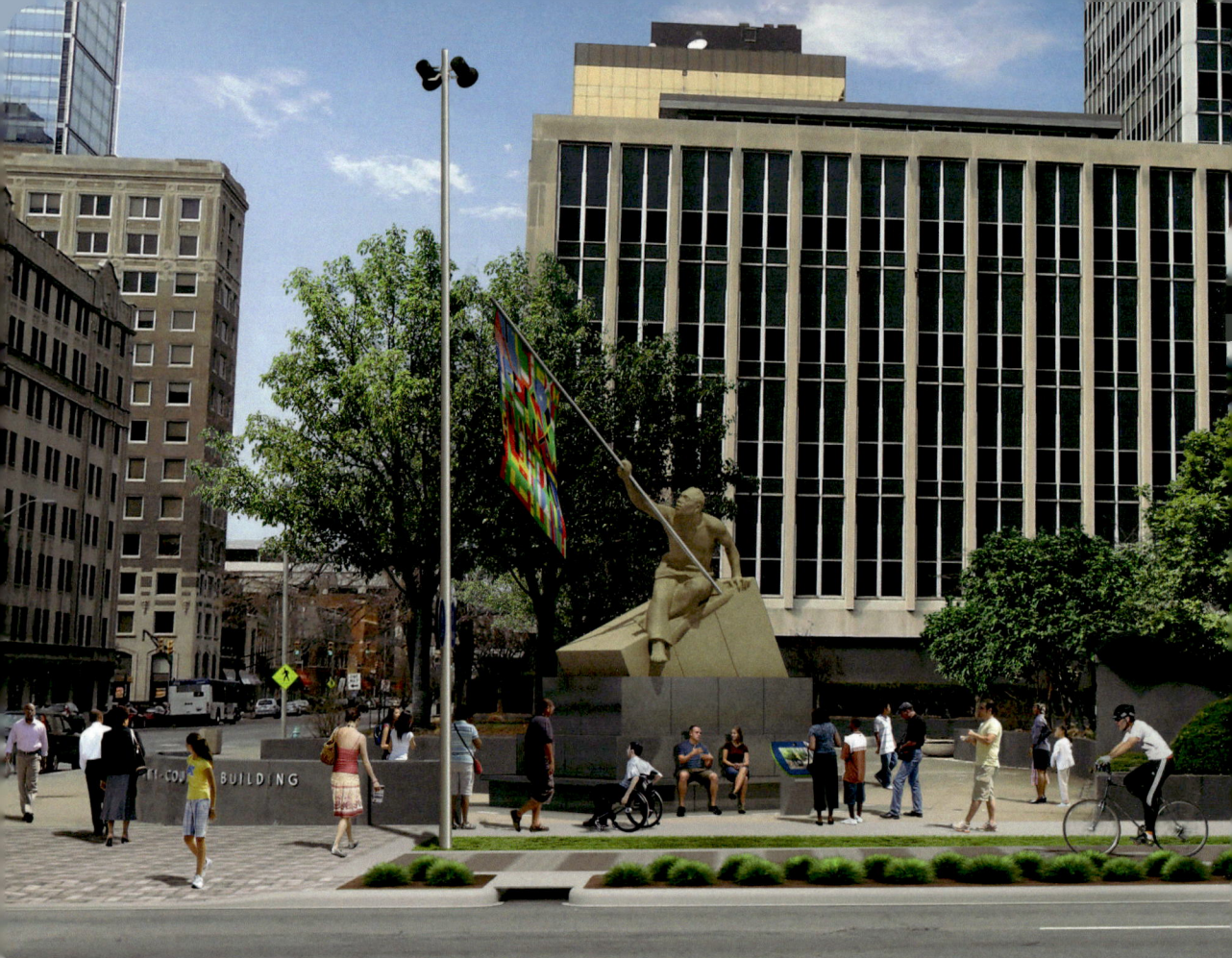

Fred Wilson, *Proposed rendering for E Pluribus Unum*, 2011.
© Fred Wilson. Photograph courtesy the artist.

cascade of lights, a ridiculous convolution of mythic forms. Wilson's plan was to free the slave figure, who amounts to a minor detail in this heroic holiday mess, and represent him individually in a nearby public square, tilting his plinth, leveling his pose, and placing in his hand a giant flag of African liberation rather than the broken chains that forever retain the imprimatur of racist bondage.

The Soldiers and Sailors Monument memorializes Indianans who participated in the Civil War, a conflict that shaped many of the enduring forces in American life, not the least of which are Memorial Day (first celebrated in Charleston by African Americans who carefully buried Union soldiers), federal cemeteries (such as Arlington, established in Confederate General Robert E. Lee's front yard), and the ideological notion, consecrated in President Lincoln's Gettysburg Address—a dedication speech for one such cemetery—that male Americans are slaughtered, dismembered, and destroyed in a transfiguration serving the enduring spirit of the nation. Their bodies are laid into an ongoing cycle of life and death that stretches from "our fathers" toward a struggled-for future, from "fourscore and seven years ago" to a singular, embattled forever. These are specific bodies, but abstracted through violence to signify the timeless principle of liberty. This mythic temporality accumulates in the monument, which eventually accrued commemorative status beyond the Civil War to encompass the

Revolutionary War, the War of 1812, the Mexican-American War, and the Spanish-American War. This temporality also shaped a popular outcry of resistance to Wilson's proposal from a group of African Americans in Indianapolis, who felt that the artist was using a public site for a work that perpetuated the injuries of antebellum slavery. One slave is enough, they declared. Here, the discourse splinters into too many pieces to adequately account for in this short essay, but their valences include general problems of public art and community engagement, the specificities of a local community exhausted by their public institutions' racist practices, and the profound difficulties a history of negativity brings to representations of blackness. In the end, Wilson's project was suspended following the protests of a community whose anti-racist interests, it could be presumed, might have been in critical allegiance with the proposal. One imagines that the sculpture, placed in a park beside a courthouse, could raise crucial questions about representation in a widely legible yet appositely complex manner that interrogates racist histories, unmediated by the inside spaces of art institutions, entering into direct dialogue with the city's public performances of itself. But it never did and it never will.

Wilson's contribution to visual art has been pivotal. His work since the 1990s has articulately and fluently expressed the notion that objects of value are embedded in discourse, as is our experience of them, and that the dominant discourses through which such objects become legible are usually very concerned with race. Wilson's work demonstrates that within the institutions that manage such materials, race is not a marginal or specialized category of consideration, but, rather, a fundamental, structuring force. His ambitious public project for Indianapolis was a development of this idea, framing public viewership through the politics of visibility. These politics can be cumbersome, and while Wilson's work has helped to develop a language for managing them within visual art contexts, in the public sphere such matters often exceed our institutional terms of arbitration. I have thought of this particular work more and more while witnessing, recently to this writing, the unveiling of artist Kara Walker's outrageously noticeable public project titled *A Subtlety, or the Marvelous Sugar Baby, an Homage to the unpaid and overworked Artisans who have refined our Sweet tastes from the cane fields to the Kitchens of the New World*, 2014. The politics of visibility have informed the discussion of Walker's work, like Wilson's, since the 1990s. The artist's famously alluring and grotesque images of antebellum fantasies also engage historical appropriation, and ask viewers to recognize their own complicity in the pleasures of scopic violence and the persistence of that tradition.

Walker's *A Subtlety*—her first sculpture—was commissioned by Creative Time in New York. Situated in an abandoned Brooklyn sugar factory, it was a spectacle at a scale beyond any the artist has attempted before, and it drew a great number of visitors and received extensive press coverage. As most readers will have noticed by now, the "subtlety" is a 35-by-75-foot sphinx with a mammy head and exposed breasts and genitals. The hollow, sugarcoated figure is attended by smaller figures, boys cast in resin and sugar who hold service items. The sphinx is smirking, the boys are melting. The installation is remarkable, to say the least. A wonder to behold, like a landmark in an ancient capital, it brings together so much to think about: it emphasizes connections between mythic images, transatlantic slavery, and global economies, crude and refined materials and tastes, industry and real estate, the paradoxes of public and private, the historical situations of various sculptural integrities, and the gendered and sexualized bodies whose energies animate these forces. As in all of her work, the artist negotiates these terms by delivering a critical ambivalence that realizes form around content that can never be resolved. Importantly, the work's massive presence is predicated on its eventual destruction, as the sugar factory itself was shortly afterward torn down and will be replaced with high-rise condos (mostly of the luxurious sort, though some contested portion are to be publicly deemed "affordable"). Like the legend of Napoleon's men smashing the nose of the Great Sphinx of Giza, history is primarily an account of fantastic demolitions.

Two days before the installation opened to the public, I (not quite politely) invited myself inside with a class of graduate art students. My discussion with these attentive and experienced viewers at a nearby beer garden afterwards was instructive. There was some debate about the idea of a public, and the kind of cultivated public that has access to this work, a niche market for refined tastes, which is very different from those who might happen upon a sculpture in a public park in, say, Indianapolis. There were modernist discussions of form, considering the figurative spectacle's relationship to prevalent sculptural terms and its hindquarters' surface resemblance to an elegant Brancuşi though departing from that history in substance and size. This set of terms was placed against a deeper origin myth, the kind of Renaissance sugar figurine to which Walker's title refers. And while the group recognized the highly politicized context for all of this, there was some uncertainty about the mobilization of race, and discussion of the familiar controversies that have followed Walker's career. As is often the case in art school, there were no African American students in this group, while more than half were from somewhere other than the United States. A young Frenchman asked how the reference to Egyptian antiquity fit into the political terms. I thought it was so obvious that I glossed over an explanation. But I've thought about that question more in the weeks since, and have tried to disentangle its threads in my mind.

There is, of course, the European colonial Orientalist fantasy of ornate and arcane power. I remember the Egyptian obelisks that stand in several of Rome's great piazzas as spoils of conquest, as well as the ways the East, Near and Far, set a stage for spectacle, gendered virtuosity, and melodramatic conflict in the great Italian operas. Double this history with the black romantic notion that were it nor for slavery's genealogical obfuscations, we would all be able to identify our origins with great kings and queens of Africa. Two strands within a mythic nostalgia, one black, one white. There's the avant-gardist appropriation of extra-European influences that we know from our art history, which sought to revitalize staid white forms with less rational gestures, extracting raw materials and refining them in Western institutions. Of course, there's Sun Ra and his ilk, Afro-fantasists who used mythological images to project black power into the future. And crucially, there's the radical ambivalence found within the American slave tradition, which simultaneously expressed both Christian and politically resistant ideas through the coded language of parables and spirituals. In nineteenth-century black songs of the American South, particular attention is paid to Egypt, Pharaoh, and Moses. When one sang of Moses in the 1850s and 60s, one may have meant both the biblical figure and Harriet Tubman, the icon of the underground railroad, who facilitated the escape of slaves from south to north. That Walker's sphinx wears a kerchief on her head is an explication of all of these poetics. When taken altogether, a sweeping history of colonialism, slavery, capitalism, and the expressive forms they produce reveals the overwhelming breadth of modernity and its oversized effects on the bodies it contains, as in this subtlety, so tremendous, exceeded only by the sugar-coated factory walls that frame it.

When imagining these two works together, Wilson's invisible man and Walker's spectacular woman, I'm reminded of art historian Huey Copeland's recent book *Bound to Appear*, which addresses the work of African American artists who, in a time of newfound multicultural visibility, engaged with representations of slavery. Copeland's title perfectly articulates the contradictions of black visibility. American representation, from the Constitution to the minstrel stage and well into the present, has always been concerned with presenting black subjects, paradoxically affirming their negative status, rendering black subjecthood impossible at the same time as requiring the perpetual identification and recognition of

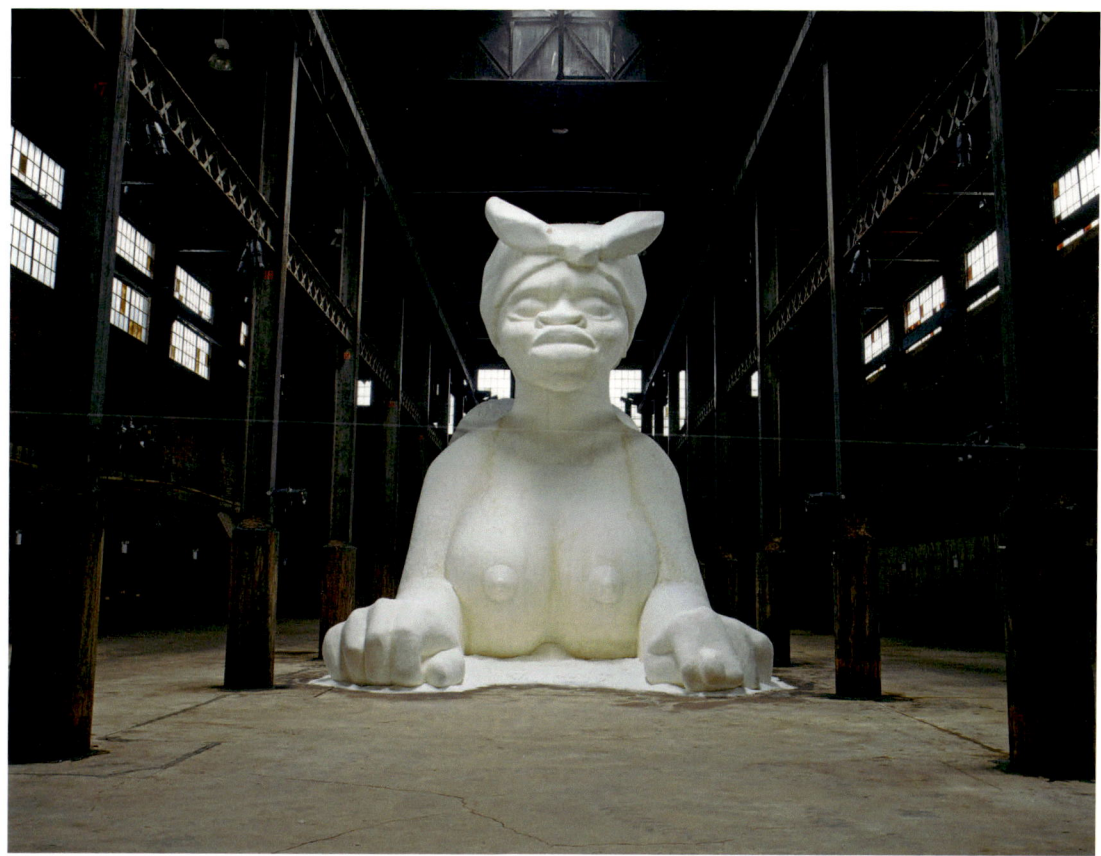

Kara Walker, *A Subtlety*, 2014.
Photo: Jason Wyche, Courtesy Creative Time.

black bodies. Further, American representations of blackness are always gendered, and often stereotypically offer a consumable woman who must be available for appropriation, in contrast to an insufficient man whose obvious instability is criminal. Walker's widely publicized sphinx and Wilson's outlawed slave play against this history. Not surprisingly, the artists' clever critical interventions have been met by public engagement that exceeds their authorial aptitudes. I observed an image of Walker's work posted on Instagram by the *National Geographic*. The thousands of comments were mostly along the uncritical lines of "Big boobies!" peppered with disapproving statements by black people offended by the work. When I saw Wilson speak about his project at the New School, he expressed deep exasperation with the outcome of his community engagement, having been ultimately thwarted by the African American citizens he had hoped his work would serve, and abandoned by city leaders unmotivated to struggle through black controversies. As these artists' works have always demonstrated, power lies not in individual objects, but in the discourse that engulfs them.

1   Copeland, Huey, *Bound to Appear: Art, Slavery, and the Site of Blackness in Multicultural America*, Chicago: University of Chicago Press, 2013.

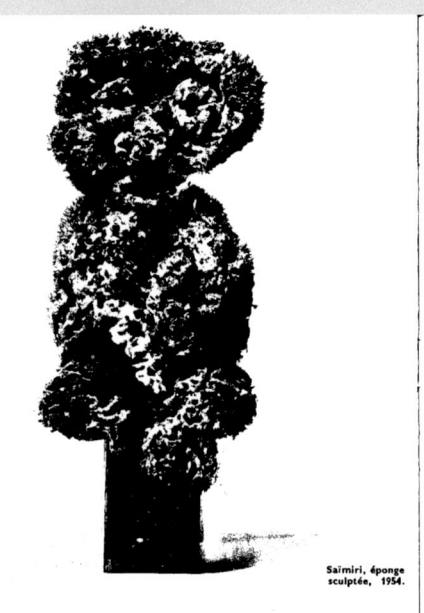

21. **FRUCTIFICATION DE LA TERRE**, 1954
73 × 60

22. **VACHE LA BELLE ALLÈGRE**, 1954
116 × 89
Galerie Rive Gauche, Paris

23. **PAYSAGE TAVELÉ AUX JAILLISSEMENTS**, 1954
65 × 50

24. **LA DANSEUSE MONGOLE**, 1954
92 × 73
Coll. particulière, Paris

DRAWINGS, etc.

1. **DAME AU CHAPEAU**, encre de Chine, 1944
19 × 28
Coll. Jean Paulhan, Paris

2. **JOE BOUSQUET AU LIT**, encre, 1947
49 × 31
Coll. Jean Paulhan, Paris

3. **DEUX ARABES ET PALMIER** (avec empreintes de pas), peinture à la colle, El Goléa, 1948
40 × 31

4. **DEUX ARABES ET DÉSERT ROSE**, peinture à la colle, El Goléa, 1948
50 × 38

5. **DEUX ARABES ET DÉSERT JAUNE**, peinture à la colle, El Goléa, 1948
55 × 46

6. **ARABES, PALMIERS, CHAMEAU**, peinture à la colle, El Goléa, 1948
55 × 46

7. **LA FÉCONDATION DES PALMIERS**, peinture à la colle, El Goléa, 1948
48 × 44

8. **CHAMEAU AU MARABOUT**, peinture à la colle, El Goléa, 1948
54 × 37

9. **ARABE ET DÉSERT**, peinture à la colle, El Goléa, 1948
50 × 38

10. **PAYSAGE AVEC PERSONNAGES**, encre de Chine, 1949
32 × 25

11. **MOISSON**, encre de Chine, 1949
32 × 25

12. **PERSONNAGE AU TURBAN**, dessin à l'encre teinté d'aquarelle, 1952
60 × 47

13. **DÉMATÉRIALISATION**, dessin à l'encre, 1952
61 × 48

Saïmiri, éponge sculptée, 1954.

Personal research material.
Courtesy Katy Siegel.

This sculpture by Jean Dubuffet is only 42 centimeters—a little over a foot—high. It is sculpted from a sponge. I found it reproduced in a catalogue for a 1955 Dubuffet show at the Institute of Contemporary Arts in London. The small pamphlet included an essay by Georges Limbour titled "Let the Material Speak for Itself", where he writes: "The perpetual and essential theme is not the object represented but the material used, such as pastes or cements, and that this material speaks in a different way according to the tools which have applied it, hollowed it out, or scratched over it. Each substance reacts differently to the hand—and to the mind—which appeals to it and displays its own resistance or willful intractability... the materials used have imposed their own demands on [Dubuffet], even going so far as to change his mood and intention while he is actually working." There are a hundred things to love about Dubuffet's sculpture and Limbour's description. First among them would be the exaltation of materiality over monumental form, the heroic figure of the artist, or rigid intellectual categories (formalism/informe). Limbour sees clearly that Dubuffet's mutual engagement with stuff is nothing less than metaphysics: "By plumbing the depths of this pictorial substance, analyzing it, transforming it, transmuting it, one can establish a link with the matter and spirit of the universe." Touch, empathy, and imagination.

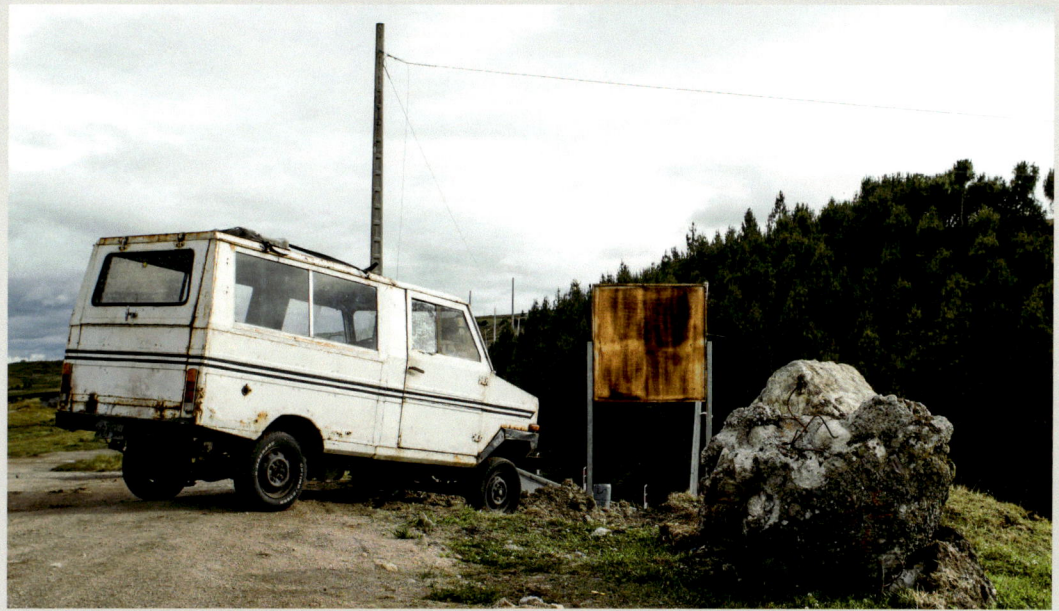

Adrián Balseca, *Medio Camino*, 2014.
Image courtesy of the artist.

The Ecuadorian "oil boom" started in 1967, when the Texaco-Gulf company drilled the now infamous oil well Lago Agrio 1: the boom catapulted the country to a search for progress that has created an ever-lasting hangover. In 1972 Aymesa, an affiliate of General Motors, launches the ANDINO, a small pick-up truck designed and assembled in Ecuador.

In *Medio Camino*, 2014, Adrián Balseca dismantles the oil tank of an ANDINO Miura 77, the last model produced during that rush of oil affluence that changed the social makeup of the country, and transports the non-functional vehicle over 2,800 miles from Quito to Cuenca, without using oil. The movement of the truck is powered by the solidarity of the people he encounters on the road, creating a poignant and poetic commentary about the unfulfilled dreams of modernity.

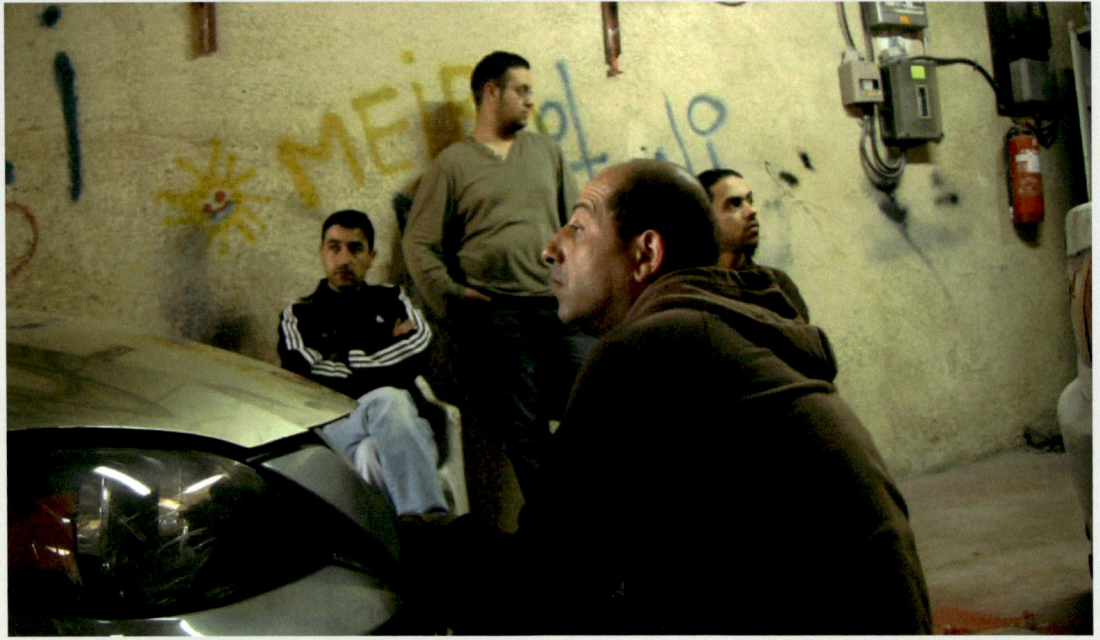

Jumana Manna, *Blessed Blessed Oblivion*, 2010.
HD Video still. Courtesy of the artist.

In 2010, I found myself in Silwan, a neighborhood in East Jerusalem where some of the earliest archaeological digs took place under the auspices of the British Palestine Exploration Fund (PEF). In 1865, Claude Conder, descendent of England's foremost eighteenth-century sculptor, Louis-François Roubiliac, led the PEF in its mission to map the Holy Land in search of material proof for biblical scripture. In its investigation and categorization of ancient objects and sites, this mission would come to establish a colonial apparatus in Palestine. I, however, was not sitting among Canaanite, Roman, Byzantine, or Mamluk ruins, but with contemporary spoils and paraphernalia collected by a young man of 25, Ahmad, and his circle of friends. I met Ahmad through my hairdresser on Salah-e-Din Street. He is what society would consider an *ars*, a rather slanderous Arabic term for "thug", "pimp", or "tough guy". This stereotype is associated with young men who have a special affinity for lustrous surfaces: the waxed body or polished rims of a car, shaved chests, gelled hair, and buffed necklaces.

Similar to movie gangsters or cowboys, *arsat* (plural) are often associated with gang culture and its mythology of underprivileged youths taking their destiny into their own hands. They give off a menacing impression, appearing to be fearless and defiant. Unlike the revolutionary, who also seeks to subvert established mores, these young men seem to have lost their compass, and are unsure how to attain the freedom they so passionately long for. They engage in escapist acts that deflect but do not defeat bourgeois culture. They are the expression of an uncertain sense of political identity among segments of Palestinian youth, and their behavior poses only a superficial threat to the established structures of power.

I tell Ahmad that I want to make a film about him. He accepts, and promises to show me his world. What would I like to see? Car thefts? Drug deals? Home gyms? Hidden cellars with stolen goods? Certainly. I follow Ahmad on his nightly adventures. He reveals to me the spaces that young men have carved out for themselves: mechanic workshops, pool-table clubs, and basement apartments in their grandmothers' houses. He tells me stories about his encounters with Israeli settlers, women, and addiction, while performing his role of manliness for me.

From Ahmad's rooftop, we see the archaeological digs in the area of Wadi Hilweh, further down the hillside, where excavations have continued off and on since the second half of the nineteenth century. Ahmad points to a tall building, on top of which a blue and white Israeli flag flaunts the structure's presence in the neighborhood. It looks as if it had been dropped by parachute onto the hill, and towers over the other residential buildings. The owners of a home that once stood at the site sold it to a Palestinian who turned out to be an agent for the ultra-right-wing Israeli settler organization Ir David, commonly called Elad (a Hebrew acronym for "to the City of David"). He took his cut and handed over the house to Elad, which demolished it and built this tower, now home to a number of Jewish families who are fenced in and protected from their surroundings by armed guards. It was one of these guards who in 2010 shot Ahmad's friend Samer Sirhan, a 32-year-old father of five.

After the occupation and annexation of East Jerusalem in 1967, Israel strengthened its control, and in 1997 the Silwan archaeological digs were transferred from the Israel Antiquities

Authority to Elad, which privatized the park where they were located, erasing the last public space in the neighborhood. Elad openly intends to displace Palestinian residents from their homes in order to secure Jerusalem as an exclusively Jewish city, justifying the expulsion by claiming that King David of the Old Testament built his palace on this spot.

During our wanderings, material details begin catching my eye: I notice the porches of the homes and steps in the alleyways. Where the limestone cladding has fallen off exterior walls, concrete has been slapped on in its place. Many houses, including their extensions, are built without permits. Not a single town-planning scheme has been approved since the occupation, making thousands of Silwan residents offenders in theory and in practice. In the evenings, some of the alleyway steps and porches become hangouts for young men. Given the lack of leisure venues, these spaces, like cars, function as stand-ins that allow for social encounters in a semi-public context. Some of the porches peer over the ancient Canaanite limestone ruins being excavated below. A broken slab of limestone veneer coating a Palestinian porch designated for demolition bears an uncanny visual relationship to a second-millennium-b.c.e. limestone pillar base that has been polished for display to religious tourists. In what seems like an inverted logic, the fallen pillars from a distant past vie with the porches in current use. Yet, despite their illegality, the porches defiantly assert their presence and endurance.

Within this contested space, connections can be drawn between the structural violence of Israeli colonialist archaeological practices in East Jerusalem and the superficial threat of the young Palestinian "thugs", not only in human actions, but also in the symbolic role of materials and objects. The young men's widespread interest in polished cars does not seem arbitrary, considering the circumstance of having had their land pulled out from under their feet. The car's aluminum body, be it in motion or in a state of repair, suggests the instability of their dwelling places. The car provides a space of intimacy and caring between men, and they extend their concern to the vehicles. Maintaining them becomes a way of escaping the daily tension of life in a constrained society. Garbage cluttering the streets reeks of the neglect of a municipality that is busy looting ancient discards. Findings are appropriated to rewrite historical memory and to buttress claims to land, serving religious belief with dubious material proof.

In the case of Silwan, I believe that mute material expression can be a means of political intervention: sculpture can reconfigure otherwise unexplored relationships by rendering them visible. Sculpture provides a physical language with which to reflect on the way materials and goods come to fashion identity and reify performances of power. The challenge is that once these artworks leave the studio and enter the public sphere, like archaeological findings removed from the earth, they slip out of the artist's control. At best, they enter public collections. In museums and galleries they are preserved and displayed, but are also subjected to what Michel Foucault called "governmentality", one of the founding principles of collections. Collections are framing powers that test the agency of sculpture. These powers, which own and interrogate objects, have purposes often at odds with the intentions with which these objects were conceived by the artist. In other words, between their production and presentation, artifacts and sculptures change in meaning as they shift from those who made them to those who view them and, finally, to those who possess them.

Ahmad pulls out a collection of stolen watches from his cupboard and tosses them on his bed. They bounce slightly and settle on the creased sheets. The fake diamonds and ticking clock hands stare silently at me. They ask me to forget about Ahmad. They don't want to be a parody of his lost time. They want to be appreciated and used for what they are, maybe even put on display in an art show. They want their tempo to be felt again, outside the wooden prison of this cupboard. But I can't hold back; I want to know more about their journey too. I ask, "Ahmad, who did you steal these watches from?"

This text followed Manna's solo exhibition, *Menace of Origins*, at SculptureCenter from 2 March–12 May 2014.

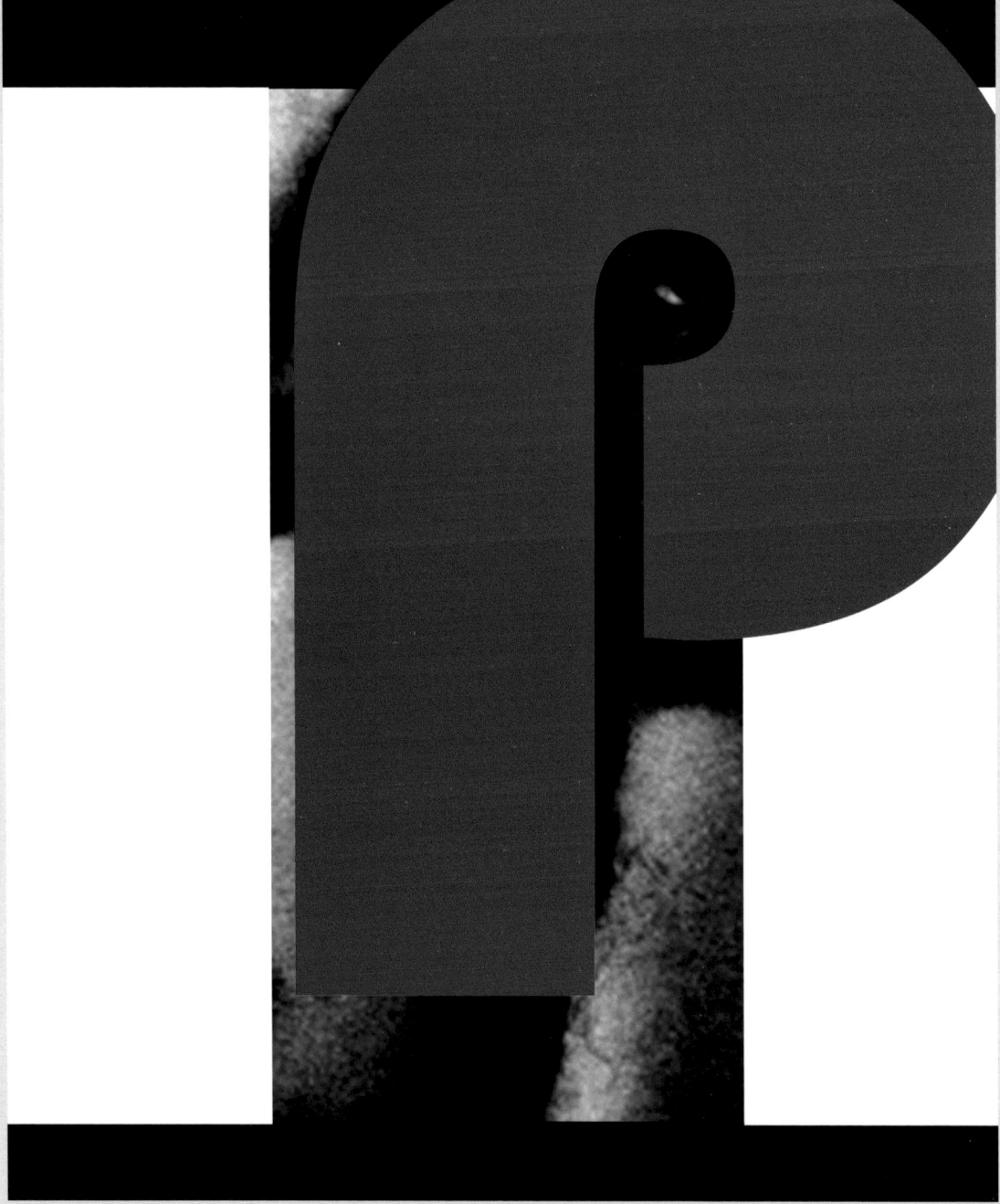

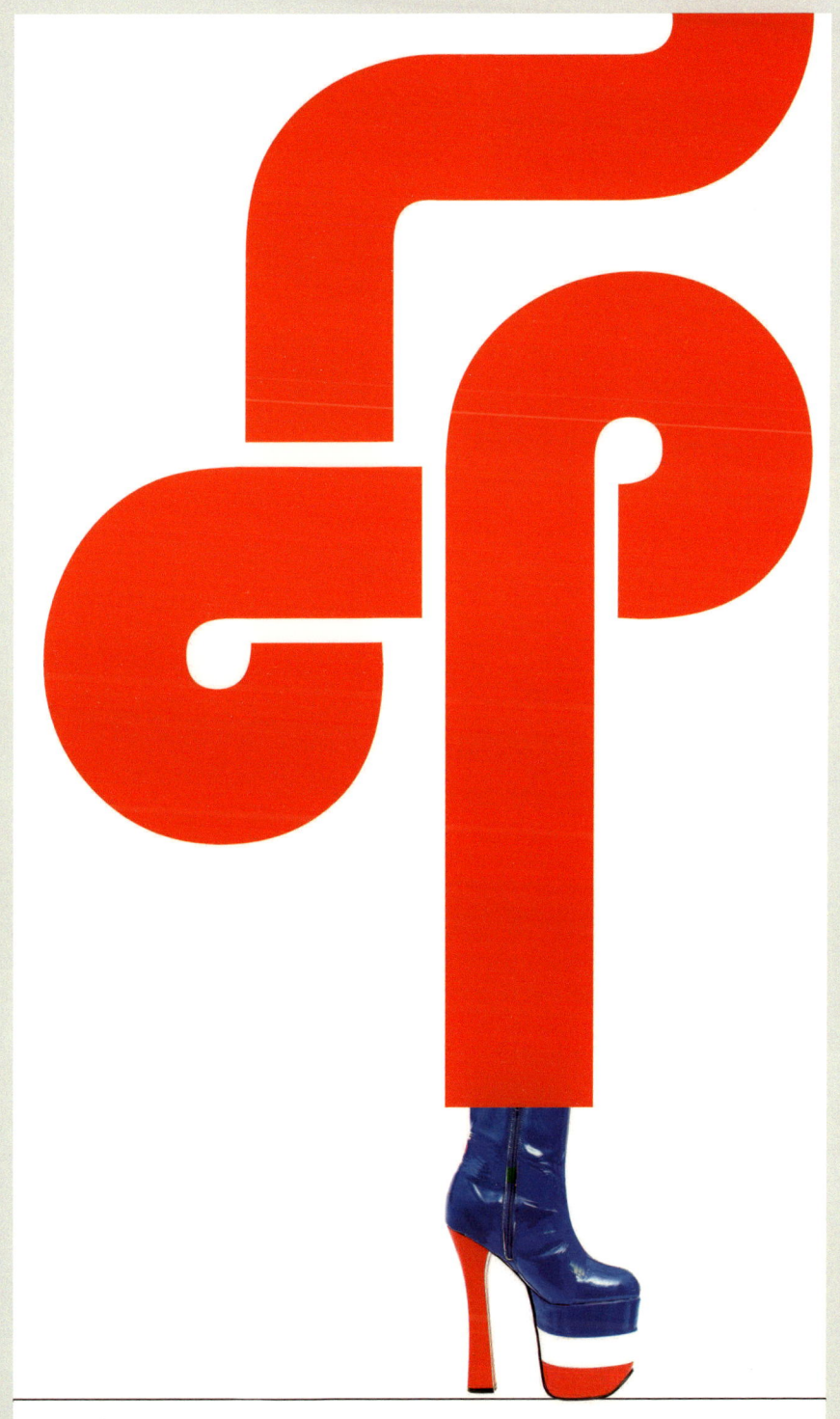

Shelter me in your pavilion
Give me respite in your tent

Grant me relief
I am in distress
My eyes are wasted by vexation
My substance and body spent in sorrow
My years are spent in groaning
My strength fails
My limbs waste away

I am the particular butt of my neighbors
I am a horror to my friends
Those who see me on the street avoid me

I am put out of mind like the dead
I am like an object given up for lost
I hear the whisperings of many

Disease plots to take my life
Sovereign powers collude
My fate is in your hands
Save me from my enemies and pursuers

Show favor to your companion
Deliver me
Let me not be disappointed when I call you
Let the wicked be disappointed
Let lying lips be stilled

Abundant is the good

Shelter me in your pavilion

As long as I said nothing my limbs wasted away from
my anguished roaring all day long

Remember me
You are my shelter

You preserve me from distress
You surround me with the joyous shouts of protest

Enlighten us
Show us which way to go
Offer counsel

My eye is on you; don't be a senseless ass

Many are the torments
Surround us with favor

Love what is right and just
Let every deed be loyal
The earth is full of faithful care

The ocean waters heap up like a mound

All the inhabitants of the city feel dread

From this dwelling place we gaze on all the inhabitants
of every city in every nation that ever was, that currently
stands, that ever will be—for we are become concrete

Fashion the hearts of all who discern with care
Kings are not delivered by a large force
Warriors are not saved by strength
Promises are a false hope for deliverance; for all their
power they provide no escape

Sustain us in absentia
Save us from our finality in oblivion

Lions have been reduced to starvation
Sustain us in our hunger
Let us taste the goodness of your portion

Here was a lowly person who called
Who listened?

Who delivered me from my troubles?

Teach me what it is to fear
Who desires years of good fortune?
Seek amity and pursue it
May your ears be attentive to my cry

We cry out, and who hears?
Save us from our troubles

The path is slippery
Rest here among the brokenhearted
Keep our bones intact, let not one of them be broken
Let those who see my life be frustrated and put to
shame
Let those who plan to harm me fall back in disgrace
Without cause they dug a pit for me

Malicious witnesses appear who question me about
things I do not know

My dress was sackcloth
I kept a fast

I walked about and you were my friend
You were bowed with gloom, like one mourning for his
mother

When we stumbled they gleefully gathered, I do not
know why

The past tears me without end

Rescue me
Let not my treacherous enemies rejoice over me, or
those without reason wink their eyes

Wake, arouse yourself for my cause
May those who rejoice at our misfortune be frustrated
and utterly disgraced
May those who vaunt themselves over me be clad
in shame

Let me not be bitter
Let me taste the goodness of repasts
Shelter us in the shadows of these wings
Let us feast on the rich fare of this tent
Let us drink at this refreshing stream

Bestow your loyal care on us
Let not the foot of the arrogant man tread on me
Here lie the fallen, thrust down, unable to rise

Do not be vexed by evil men
Do not be incensed by wrongdoers

Grant us the desires from your heart
Be patient
Do not be vexed, it can only do harm

Delight in abundant well-being
The dead do not begrudge you your good fortune

Be concerned for the needs of the blameless; our
portion lasts forever

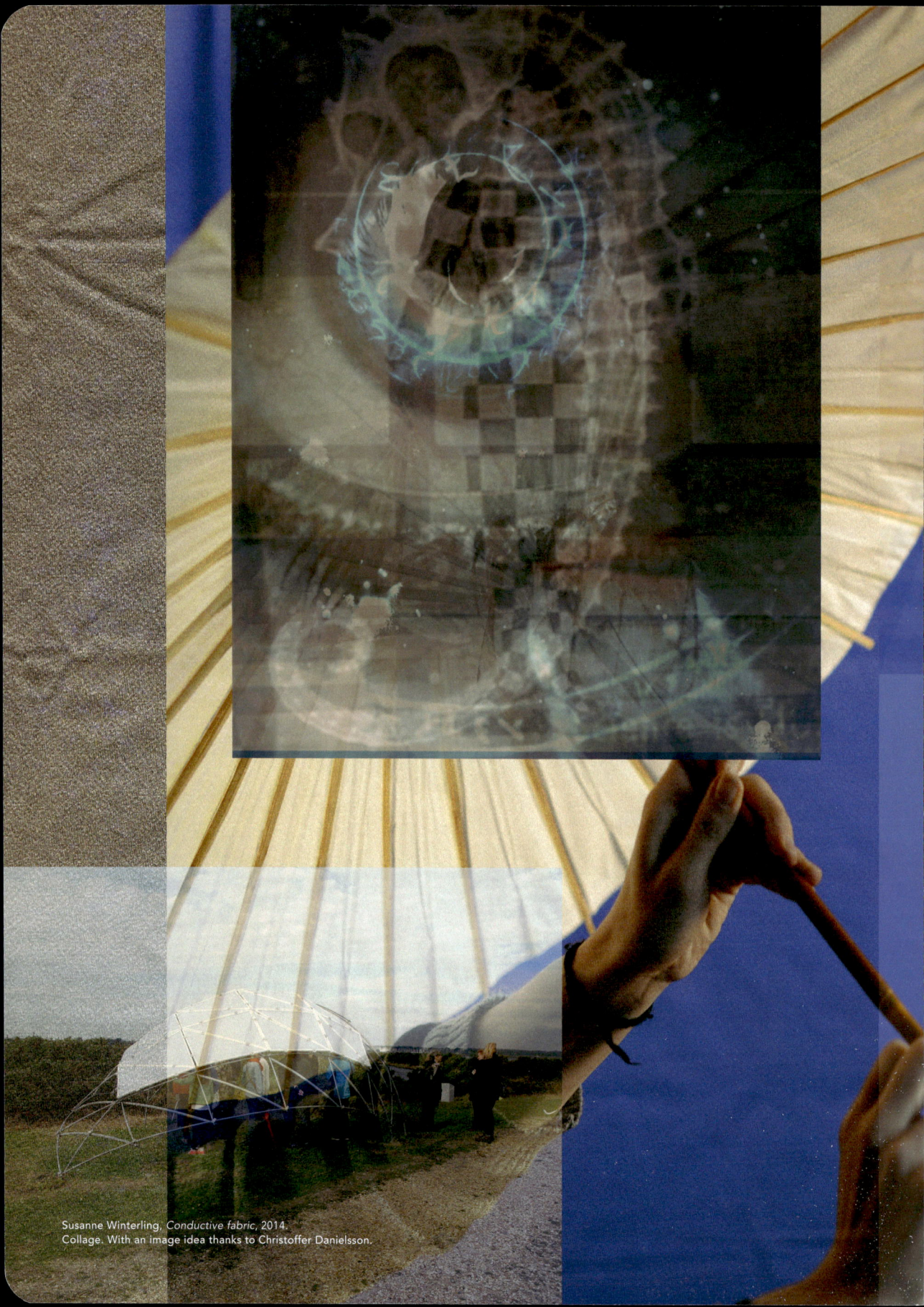

Susanne Winterling, *Conductive fabric*, 2014.
Collage. With an image idea thanks to Christoffer Danielsson.

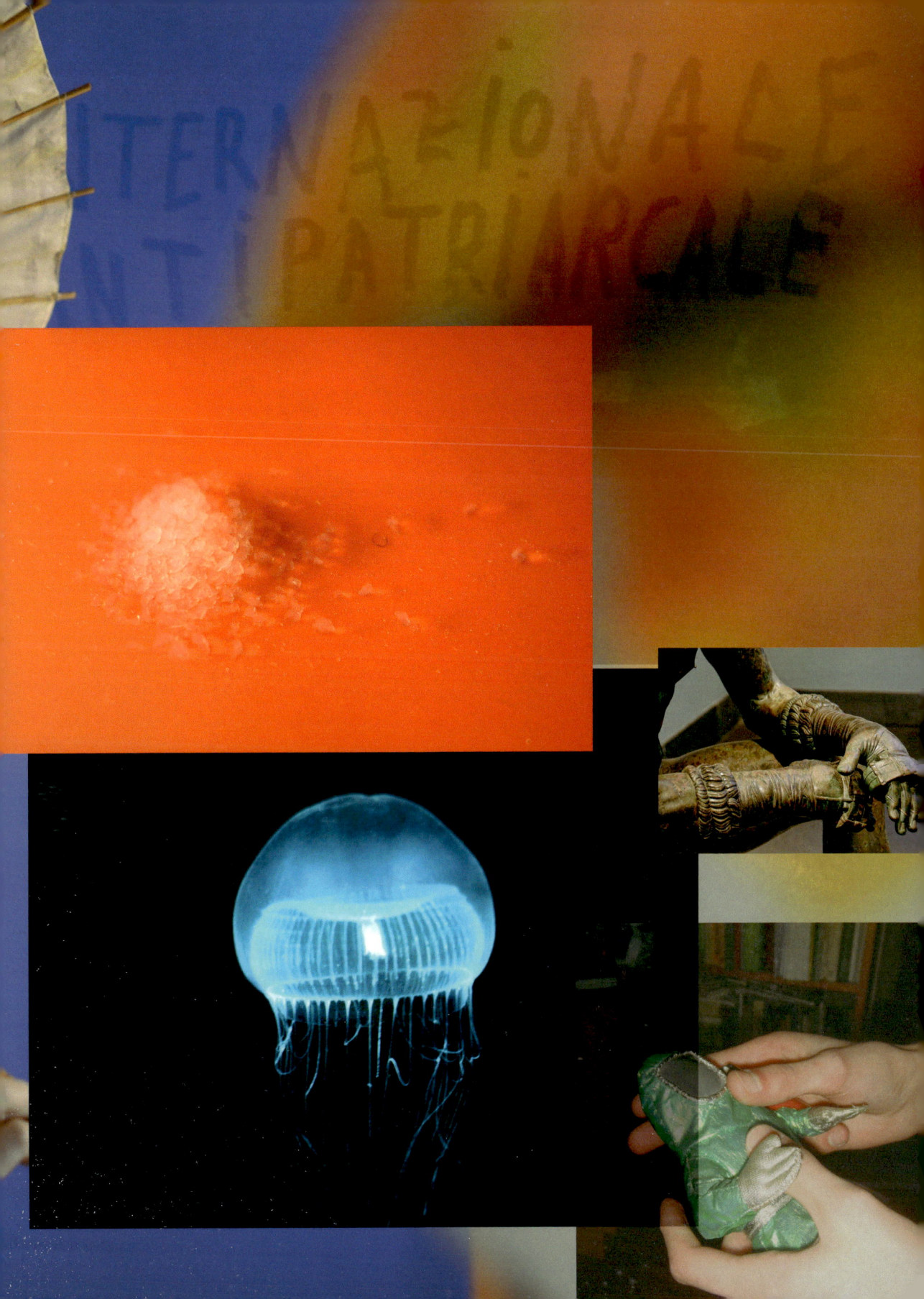

It goes without saying that commissioning artists to create temporary sculpture for public space is tricky business. There are complex circumstances, the most obvious of which are the pragmatic issues of public safety, weather conditions, and vandalism. A more complicated matter is evaluating the power of an object in relationship to its surroundings: the skyscrapers, traffic, LED screens, smartphones, and myriad personal concerns that infiltrate the viewer's experience. Sculpture does not move easily from the gallery to the street—its formal considerations are very different when it is created for the public realm. As such, publicly sited sculpture raises an urgent question about the power and efficacy of the art object to reach beyond the insular discourses of the art world.

The public sphere is a frontline for an attention economy that increasingly accelerates its demands on the passerby. In this economy, city spaces designated for sculpture tend to occupy the edge of our field of vision: plazas are lost between flagship stores, green space is stretched along the office commute, and everywhere is a space for advertising. One of the luxuries of the gallery space is its ability to frame both the object and the viewer, excluding exterior (real life) distractions and focusing our attention on the inherent merits and formal considerations of sculpture.

Following the model of attention economics, which employs a set of advertising strategies known as AIDA—Attention, Interest, Desire, and Action—the power of sculpture in the public realm lies, first and foremost, in its ability to attract the viewer's attention. We have only to think of Olafur Eliasson's waterfalls across Manhattan's East River, Jeff Koons's enormous shiny balloon dogs, Anish Kapoor's seductive mirror surfaces, or Louise Bourgeois' giant spiders to see how these well-known artists use scale, transformation, and expectation to call our attention to order.

Still, the use of spectacle in public art can be seen as something of a cheap trick associated with AIDA's negative intentions—consumer capitalism, manipulation, and propaganda of all persuasions. Yet I would argue that it is worth taking a closer look at the seduction at play. Engaging the spectacular within sited sculpture can be a way to re-engage the viewer, and many of the most successful public works unabashedly use this technique. The surface of our public sphere—particularly in urban settings—requires spectacle to help us distinguish between different kinds of power, granting it to the viewer in ways the gallery space cannot. For *Discovering Columbus*, 2012, Tatzu Nishi used four-story scaffolding to raise a temporary New York apartment, allowing for an up-close and personal experience of the statue of Columbus at Columbus Circle, and completely transforming the view of a New York commercial center at the same time. Similarly, Katharina Fritsch's recent 4th Plinth commission, *Hahn/Cock*, 2013, transformed London's Trafalgar Square with an oversized rooster—4.7 meters high—painted a deep matte blue. The sculpture is iconic and colorful eye candy for visitors and locals alike. After capturing viewers' attention and drawing them in, the object exposes numerous double entendres: a cock with tail feathers mocking the National Gallery; an artist flipping the bird at the masculine posturing of Nelson's Column; and the classical symbolism of regeneration or rebirth.

Objects that invite us to look closely are powerful. They are pointing devices, they tell us what to look at, but they also show us *how* to look. By creating that shift, the power of the viewer emerges in relationship to the sculpture. What does this object leave us with? What, specifically, do we see or experience that shows us what we might have missed on the surface of our public sphere, what we might have taken for granted or simply ignored?

In this way, the object has both performative and potential power. The sculpture invites a second look that penetrates the scrim of the city. It is far too big, or too small, it is in the wrong place, or its function or material is unexpected. Like a street performer, it dances, performs tricks, and points to itself to catch our attention. The sculpture becomes powerful in its ability to reach beyond the discourse of the art object to refocus the attention of the audience onto itself. Sculpture in public spaces has the power to point at *us* and show us the world we live in. Calling attention to higher goals, it reproaches us for our inattention and encourages us to see more clearly what might already exist in the city around us.

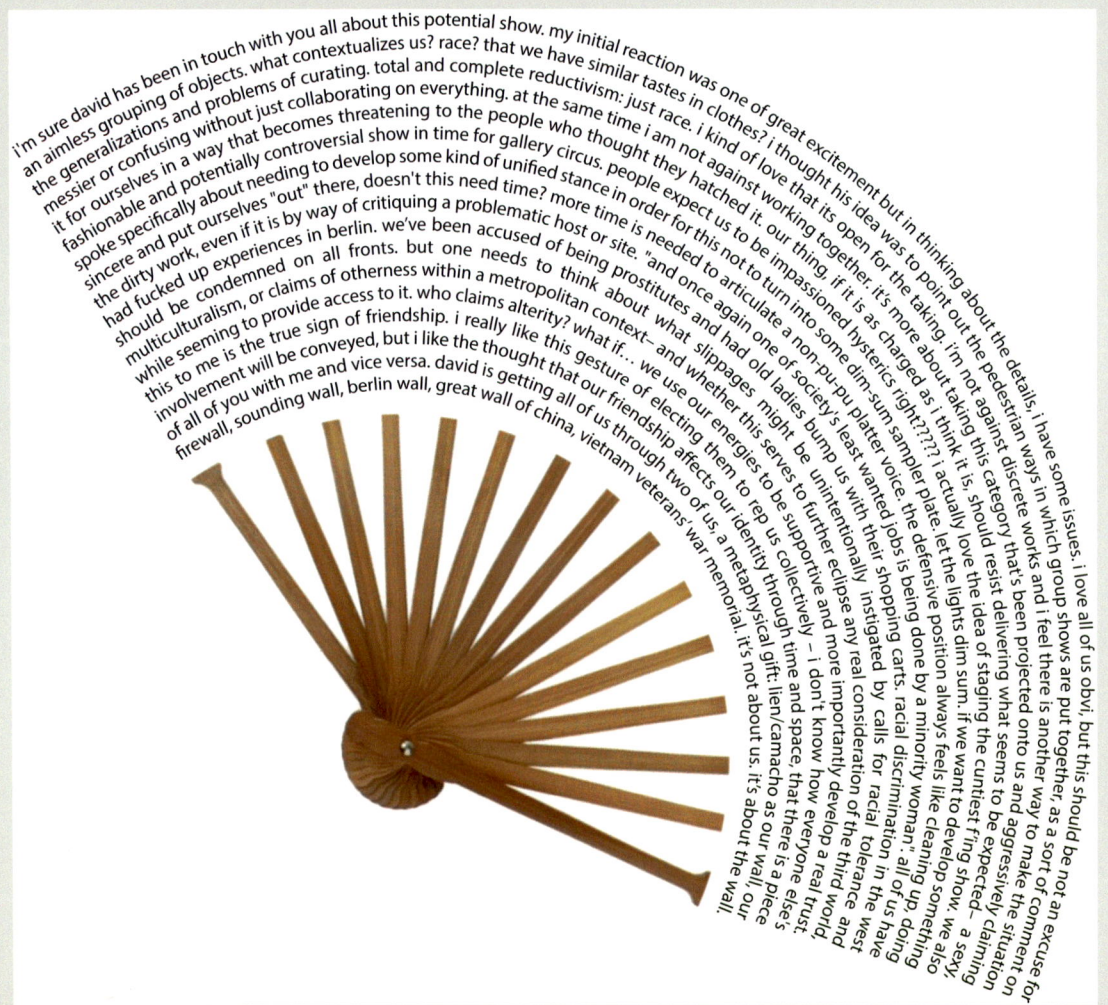

i'm sure david has been in touch with you all about this potential show. my initial reaction was one of great excitement but in thinking about the details. i have some issues. i love all of us obvi, but this should be not an excuse for an aimless grouping of objects. what contextualizes us? race? that we have similar tastes in clothes? i thought his idea was to point out the pedestrian ways in which group shows are put together, as a sort of comment for the generalizations and problems of curating. total and complete reductivism: just race. i'm not against taking this category that's been projected onto us and aggressively claiming it for ourselves in a way that becomes threatening to the people who thought they hatched it. our thing, if it is as charged as i think it is, should resist delivering what seems to be expected— a sexy messier or confusing without just collaborating on everything. at the same time i am not against working together. i actually love the idea of staging the cuntiest f'ing show. we also fashionable and potentially controversial show in time for gallery circus. people expect us to be impassioned hysterics right????? i let the lights dim sum. if we want to develop something spoke specifically about needing to develop some kind of unified stance in order for this not to turn into some dim-sum sampler plate. the defensive position always feels like cleaning up, doing sincere and put ourselves "out" there, doesn't this need time? more time is needed to articulate a non-pu-pu platter voice. the shopping carts. racial discrimination: all of us have the dirty work, even if it is by way of critiquing a problematic host or site. "and once again one of society's least wanted jobs is being done by a minority woman'. all of us have had fucked up experiences in berlin. we've been accused of being prostitutes and had old ladies bump us with their racial tolerance in the west should be condemned on all fronts. but one needs to think about what slippages might be unintentionally instigated by calls for racial tolerance in the west multiculturalism, or claims of otherness within a metropolitan context— and whether this serves to further any real consideration of the third world. while seeming to provide access to it. who claims alterity? what if... we use our energies to be supportive and more importantly develop a real trust. this to me is the true sign of friendship. i really like this gesture of electing them to rep us collectively – i don't know how everyone else's involvement will be conveyed, but i like the thought that our friendship affects our identity through time and space, that there is a piece of all of you with me and vice versa. david is getting all of us through two of us, a metaphysical gift. lien/camacho as our wall, our firewall, sounding wall, berlin wall, great wall of china, vietnam veterans' war memorial. it's not about us. it's about the wall.

Mathew Berliner Mauer, 2014.
Amy Lien & Enzo Camacho
Representing: Lisa Jo, Margaret Lee, Amy Lien & Enzo Camacho,
Carissa Rodriguez, Anicka Yi, and Amy Yao
Courtesy of the artists and Mathew Gallery, Berlin.

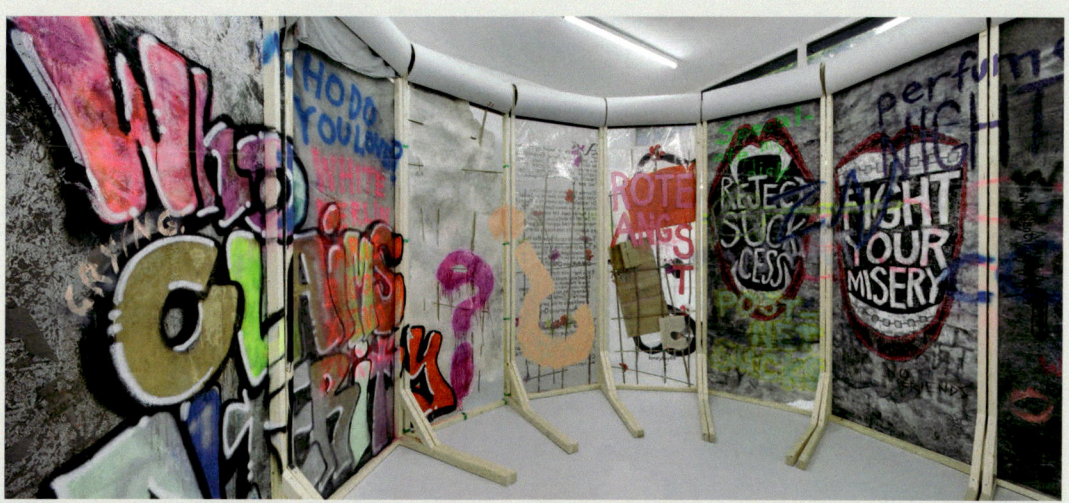

Mathew Berliner Mauer, 2014.
Amy Lien & Enzo Camacho
Representing: Lisa Jo, Margaret Lee, Amy Lien & Enzo Camacho,
Carissa Rodriguez, Anicka Yi, and Amy Yao
Courtesy of the artists and Mathew Gallery, Berlin.

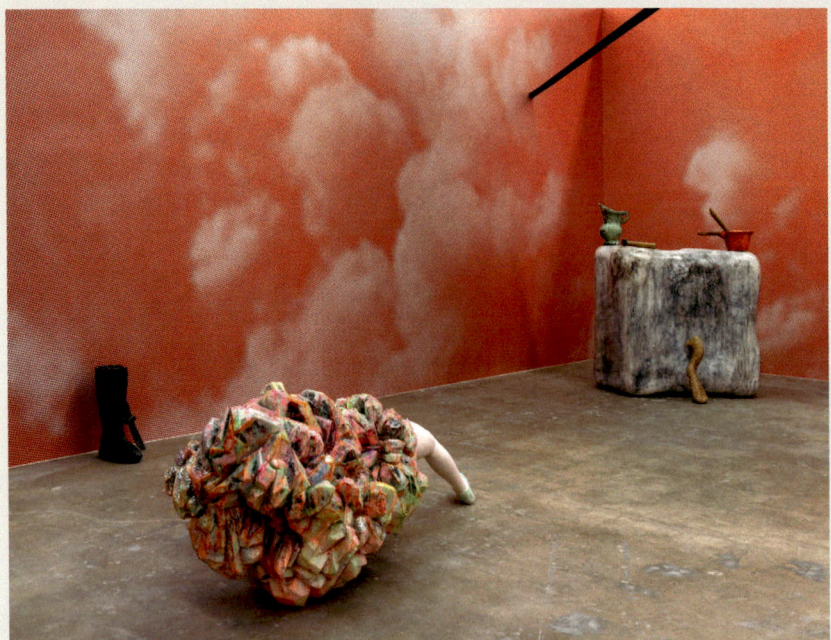

Naufús Ramírez-Figueroa, *Props for Eréndira*, 2014.
Mixed media installation, dimensions variable.
Courtesy of Gwangju Biennale Fondation.

If in the twentieth century the supposedly superior mode of abstraction prevailed over figuration in a contest that saw its coldest moment in the postwar period, in the twenty-first century Postmodernism and its factions have found renewed strength in narrative. Power-asserting figuration ended at the beginning of the twentieth century with the deconstruction of the monument and in less than a hundred years we ventured into the void of abstraction, only to return disappointed by the sterility of rationality. In the last several decades, art production has steered away from the clinical exercises of minimalism and beyond to rediscover narrative subjects that not only recount, but also incite and provoke.

It is significant that during this time of unrest and change, the human figure should once again become the leading carrier of meaning and action. Whether realistic, symbolic, or even absent, the body in representation carries out what the mind cannot, thus enacting a reconciliation with art's magical origins. At the same time, the developing exploration of matter and its agency defies the substantial and symbolic meaning of sculpture and continues to question the solidity of the monument.

Current sculptural practices, particularly in relation to a critical engagement with power, depict the human and other bodies from the perspective of an intelligent, emotional, and able organism itself. Uruguayan writer Eduardo Galeano coined the term *sentipensante* to refer to a body that thinks and feels in equal measure but, it should be added, is also able to carry out actions. Indeed, it is no coincidence that performance has acquired a determinant role within artistic practice and that the public domain, as the historically symbolic space for power, and monuments, is a preferred venue.

It is within this framework that Naufús Ramírez-Figueroa, a Guatemalan migrant in Canada, poses the body at the center of a multimedia practice in which he questions accepted notions of social, human, and historical responsibility. Straightforwardly figurative, the characters in Ramírez-Figueroa's sculptural practice stand for large yet profoundly personal stories. The materials the artist chooses, appropriately, are not the concrete, cast bronze, or marble apt for grand and expectedly enduring national narratives. Instead, he uses glue, fabric, resin, and various types of clay to create the guts of people and animals alike. In *Props for Erendira*, 2014, his recent large-scale sculptural installation for the 10th Gwangju Biennale, characters and objects, casted in Styrofoam and covered in pigments and resin, loosely recreate the story of a girl who has accidentally burnt down her grandmother's house and is forced into prostitution to pay for the damage. In *Bitch on a Bent Palm Tree*, 2011, a dog with the head of Lynndie England stands on the phallic trunk of a papier-mâché tree that is suspended horizontally in space. In both cases, the figures mutely but pointedly embody human experience.

Simultaneous with his sculptural work, Ramírez-Figueroa has developed a performance practice that focuses on the body as a means as well as an end in itself. The body — aesthetically non-normative, queer-feeling, political — is often his own, as the producer of the action and at the same time its most real representation and, in its gentle, imperfect, and mimetic power, an ultimate monument to the intimate. The works consist of rather simple, highly lyrical actions that usually involve the symbolic transformation of the body. In *Rainbow Action (after Cezary Bodzianowski and the lost dreams of socialism)*, the artists reenacts the classic Bodzianowski performance in which the Polish artist paints his body and stages a rainbow between his bathtub and toilet. In a more recent performance on the occasion of a solo exhibition at Castello di Rivoli in Turin, Ramírez-Figueroa pierced his left arm with feathers in an allegory of fear, queernesss, and death as represented by a one-winged man.

Rooted in both a traditional notion of sculpture and newer object- and action-related practices — though informed by the current concern with material culture — every character and object in Ramírez-Figueroa's work is capable of telling many stories. Flesh, the first and last human material, returns the monument to the body, restoring power to its original source. Soft sculptures, then, refer not only to the materials they are made of — including flesh — but also to the discourse they contribute to: they are fluid, organic articulations of the personal struggle with worldly power and its representation.

NOT WHAT WE SEE

IN

THE SCULPTURES

BUT HOW

THE SCULPTURES

MIGHT

ENABLE US

TO SEE

EVERYTHING ELSE

OBJECTS

CAN TEACH US HOW TO SEE OTHER

OBJECTS

AND HOW TO SEE OTHER

BODIES

AND HOW TO SEE OUR OWN

BODIES

RECOGNIZING

RENEWED

POSSIBILITIES

IN ONE ANOTHER

AND OURSELVES

WHAT

IS ACTUALLY

HOW

AND

WE LEARN FROM

THE THINGS

THEMSELVES

SHAPE

LIGHT

ARCHITECTURE

BLANKNESS

SILENCE

IS A TOOL

TO UNCOVER

THE POSSIBLE

                                                    IN EXCESS OF THE REAL

                                                    ABSTRACTION

TRANSFORMATION

                                                    I CAN MAKE WORK ABOUT

WHAT I CAN'T MAKE WORK ABOUT

                                                    SEEING

BODIES

                                                    WITHOUT

DEMANDING TO KNOW

                                                    WHERE THEY CAME FROM

OR WHERE THEY ARE GOING

A TRANSPARENT WALL

                                                    THROUGH WHICH

IDEAS

                                                    ARE

ACTUALITIES

                                                    CEILING

FLOOR

                                                    A VIRTUAL

DOUBLE   DOUBLE

ILLUSIONS

                                                    AS REAL AS

FACTS

                                                    FACTS

AS EPHEMERAL AS

                                                    ILLUSIONS

BETWEEN ME AND THE OBJECT

                                                    A RELATIONSHIP OF USE

YES   NO

(Repeat, with roles reversed)

Note: This script for two readers was adapted from Gordon Hall, "Object Lessons: Thinking
Gender Variance Through Minimalist Sculpture", *Art Journal* 72 (4), winter 2013, p. 46.

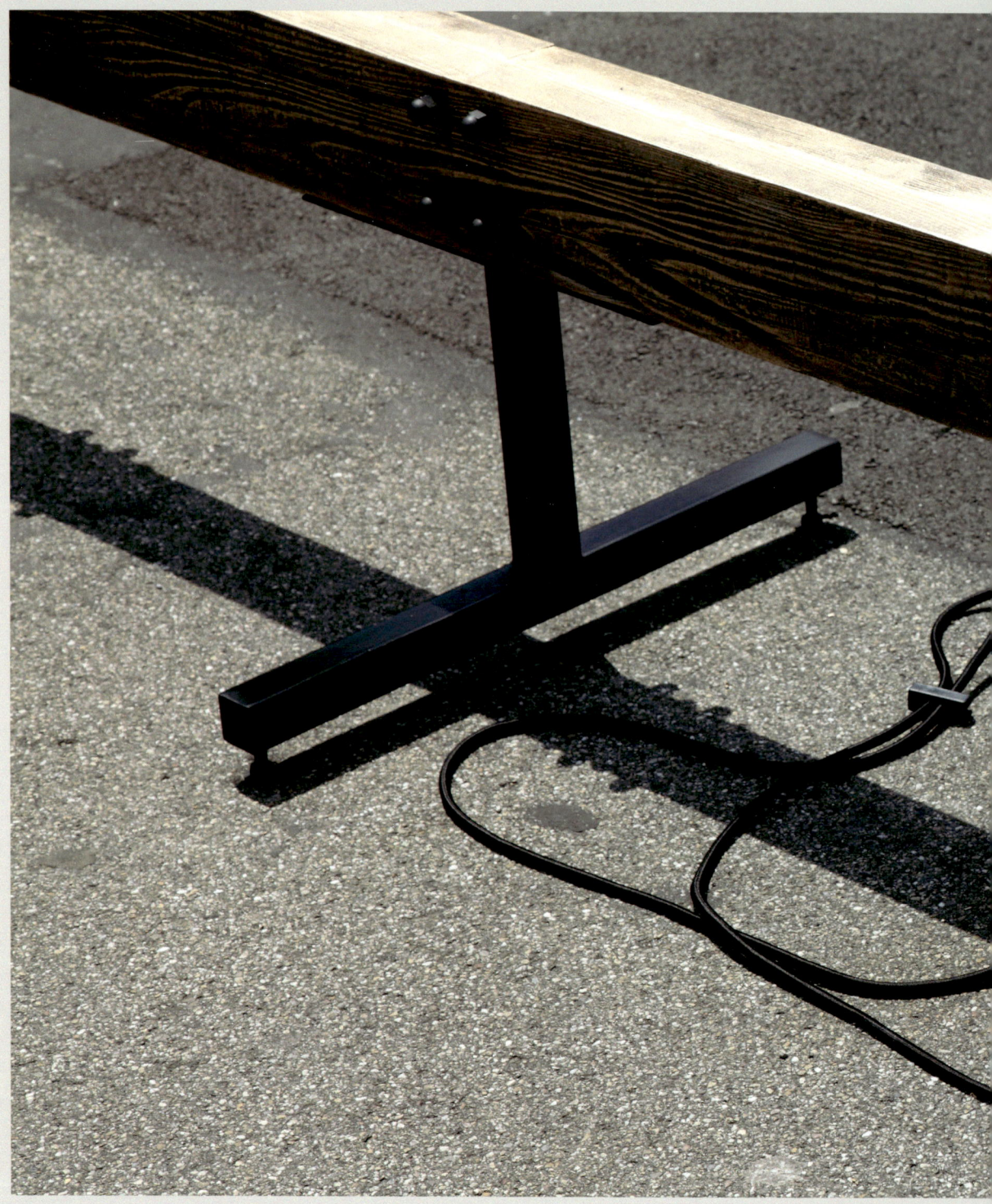

Tom Burr, *Straightness*, detail, 2013.
Courtesy of the artist and Bortolami, New York.

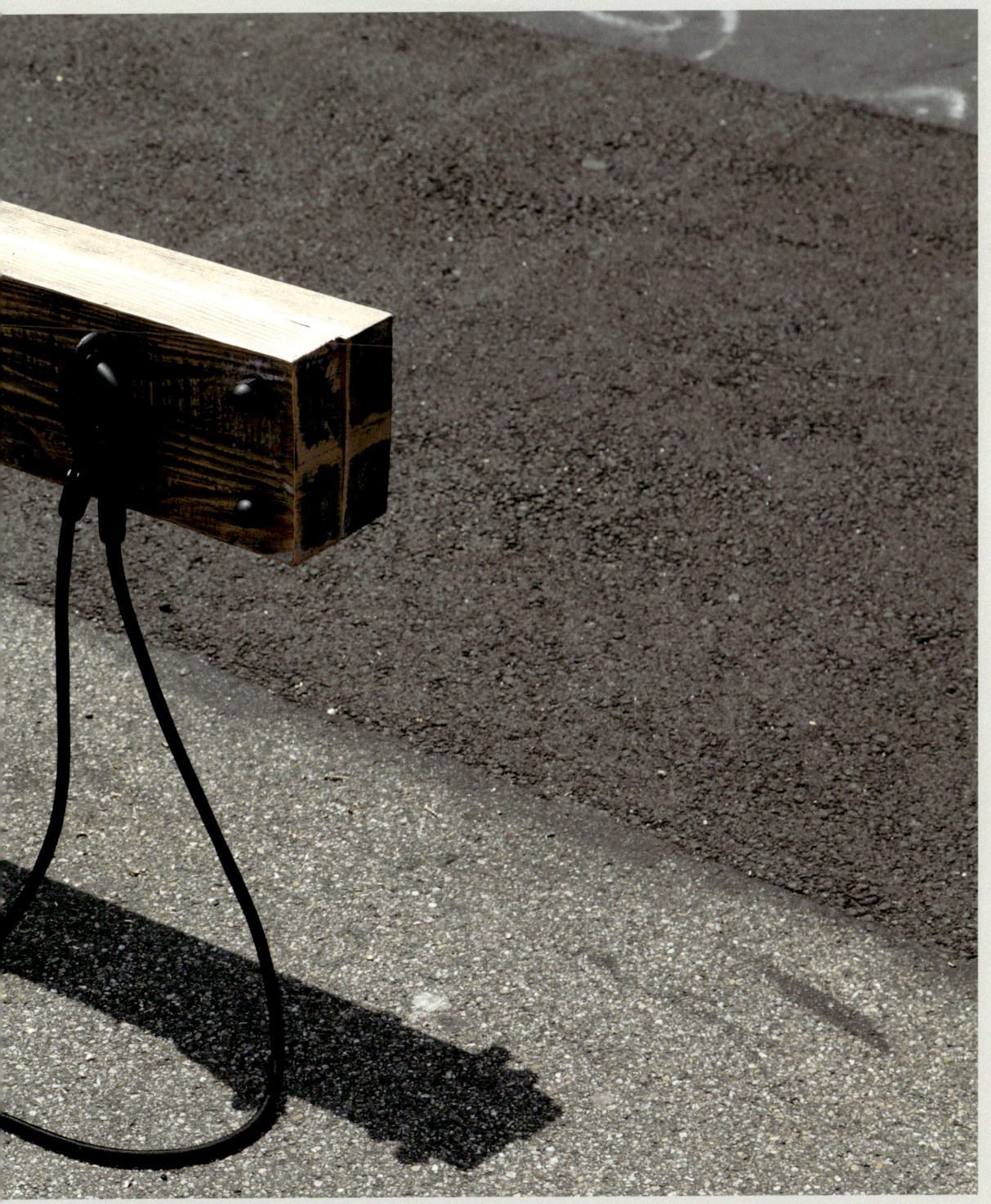

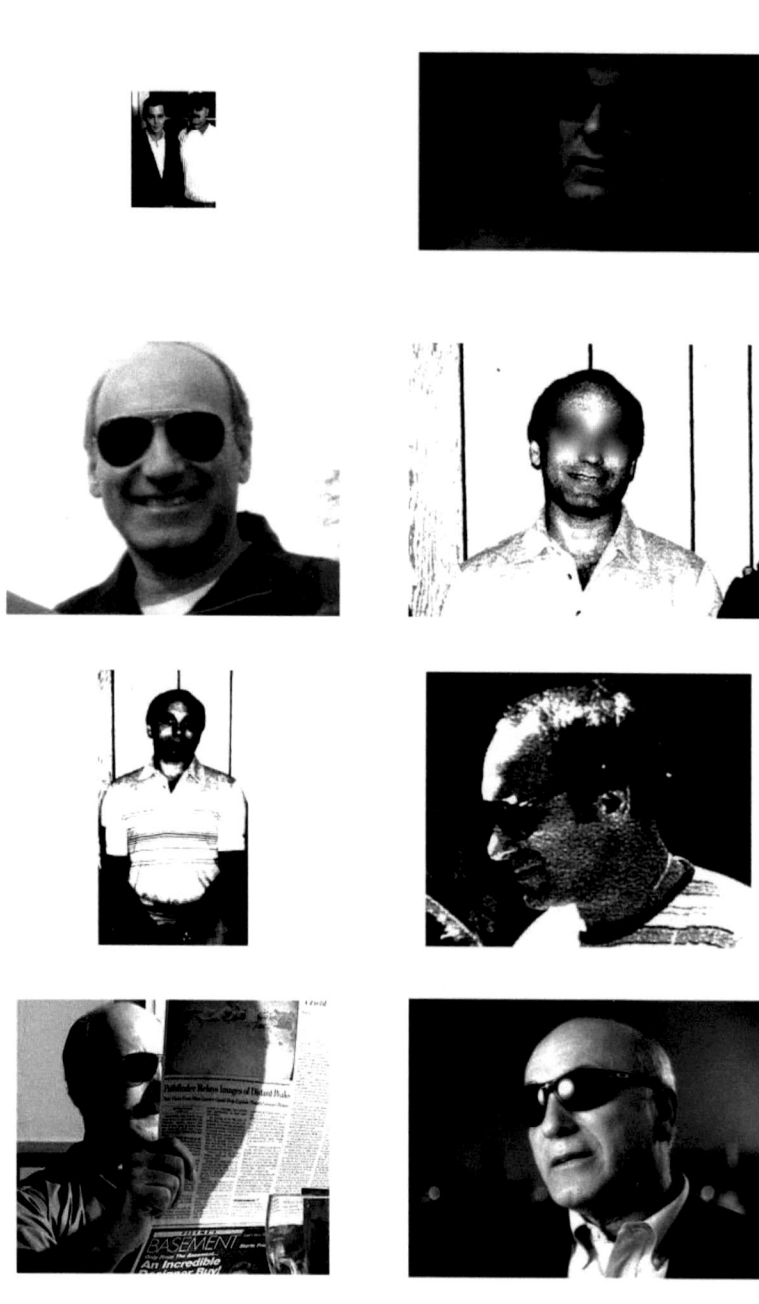

Compilation of Joseph D. Pistone aka Donnie
Brasco's pictures available online in 2007.

05.05.07   ROSSELLA---RECEIVED YOUR EMAIL----LOOKING
           FORWARD TO SEEING YOU ITALY FOR INTERVIEW
           BEST----JOE

01.06.07   ROSSELLA-------SENT YOU 2 VIDEO TAPES--ONLY
           ONES I COULD FIND-----REGARDS JOE

06.06.07   HELLO ROSSELLA-------TAPES ARE FROM FLA AND
           LOS VEGAS------HOLD ON TO THEM UNTIL I SEE
           YOU----JOE

25.06.07   Rossella----good day------re photos----#1 I am on left
           #2 I am in middle #3 I am on left others in photos are
           gangsters Best joe

09.08.07   Call me any time Monday----JOE

21.08.07   Rossella-----I will send you the name I will be using to travel
           under----it will be the name to get the airline tickets and
           hotel in.   Also will send you airport I will be leaving and
           returning TO… THANK YOU (PS---NAME WILL NOT
           BE PISTONE)

04.10.07   GOOD MORNING---TICKET IN NAME OF JOSEPH D.
           ██████ SUNGLASSES---YES JACKET--43 REGULAR
           PANTS--WAIST-35 LENGHTH--33 SHIRT--NECK-15/1/2
           ARMS---34-35   YOU CAN GIVE ME MONEY IN ROME
           LOOKING FORWARD TO TRIP   BEST---JOE

04.10.07   ROSSELLA-----NO NEED TO ALERT POLICE

05.10.07   Dear Mr. Pistone, below there is the e-ticket for the flight.
           The agency didn't need to include your second name,
           I already made sure that everything is correct. Thank you
           so much. Looking forward to the film. Best regards, rossella

Email exchange between Joseph D. Pistone aka
Donnie Brasco, former FBI agent, during the making
of the film *The Undercover Man*, 2007–2008.

Working Artists and the Greater Economy (W.A.G.E.) is a New York-based activist group that focuses on regulating the payment of artist fees by non-profit art institutions, and establishing a sustainable model for best practices between cultural producers and the institutions that contract their labor.

The following text is an excerpt from the policy for W.A.G.E. Certification, a program launched in 2014 that recognizes non-profits voluntarily paying artist fees that meet a minimum payment standard. Developed in dialog with local and international arts organizations, W.A.G.E. Certification is the first model in the U.S. that sets a clear, industry-wide minimum standard for artist compensation and defines the terms on which artistic labor is contracted.

Defining the Artist Fee

An 'honorarium' is defined by Wikipedia as *a payment given for professional services that are rendered nominally without charge*, while a 'fee' is *the price one pays as remuneration for services*. A fee, while being neither a salary nor a wage, still distinguishes itself from an honorarium by being actual compensation—not a representation of compensation.

Why then, have 'artist fees' never been conceived or implemented as compensation? Unlike rental, membership, insurance, planning, or consulting fees, the artist fee is an arbitrary sum that has come to symbolize the inability or unwillingness of institutions to determine compensation based on anything resembling the actual cost of the content or services provided by artists at a rate of fair pay. By accepting the fee as a representation of compensation—essentially an excuse for not paying more—artists also accept that it is enough for institutions to represent the intention to compensate fairly, enabling the intention alone to supplant their actually doing so.

If this is to change, clarification is needed regarding what the fee is in fact compensation for. This first requires it to be untethered from the other expenses associated with mounting an exhibition or program. In other words, the first task is to define what the fee is *not*.

Basic Programming Costs and Services

The fee is not intended to cover what W.A.G.E. defines as *Basic Programming Costs and Services*. These are the baseline costs associated with mounting or executing programs as articulated by the institution's mission statement and constitute the basic services that artists can expect an institution to provide, irrespective of specific content.

As contemporary conditions of precarity increasingly necessitate that workers supply the workplace infrastructure (laptop, cell phone, mobile office) W.A.G.E. asserts that in a visual arts context the opposite is true: the institution, if nothing else, *is* the infrastructure that *cannot* be provided by the artist. Basic programming costs and services are not negotiable—they are the responsibility of the host institution and are required for certification. They include:

Provision of exhibition, performance, or projection space
Preparation of exhibition, performance, or projection space for the program
Shipping and insurance costs when necessary
Presentation infrastructure, including display equipment, exhibition furniture and lighting
Documentation of exhibition or event
Promotion of exhibition or event
Travel and accommodation when necessary
Obtaining and paying for image rights

Criteria for institutions supporting non-material practices that are not exhibition or program-based, and whose presentation or execution does not utilize physical space are in development.

Production Costs

The fee is also not intended to cover *Production Costs* which W.A.G.E. has defined as the costs associated with the production of a work on a time-limited basis, sometimes resulting from a commission by an institution. Production costs are negotiated between artist and institution and may include:

- Fabrication of work
- Specialized installation expenses above and beyond Basic Programming Costs and Services
- Studio rental
- Equipment rental
- Subcontracted labor by graphic designers, fabricators, performers, lighting designers, etc.

The coverage of production costs is not required for W.A.G.E. Certification but it is imperative that the negotiation of their coverage has no bearing on, or relationship to, the artist fee or the provision of basic programming costs and services. While in many cases it might be reasonable to expect an institution to cover production costs, W.A.G.E. elected not to make this a condition of certification because it would prohibit smaller institutions with lesser means from being certified.

W.A.G.E. recognizes the importance of small-scale institutions and the precarious conditions under which they operate, but many of the non-profits that started out in precisely this way, emerging from the alternative space movement of the early 1970s, have since evolved into mid- to large-sized institutions that no longer serve as alternatives; certainly, the risk of exhibiting unaffiliated or 'untested' artists is not exclusively their domain. Instead, artists are now more likely to receive their first institutional exhibition only after they have been 'tested' in the commercial market. With the financial and programmatic risk of supporting unaffiliated or lesser-known artists being shouldered by commercial galleries, the non-profit must now distinguish itself by operating as a small museum or *kunsthalle*, providing infrastructure, resources, and commissioning projects on a comparable or larger scale. Because the non-profit's ability to cover these costs is limited by how much money it can raise through traditional funding streams, they are increasingly being subsidized by the commercial galleries that represent affiliated artists when they exhibit in non-profits.

Non-profit and for-profit economies are already in dangerous overlap when collectors and dealers serve as board members where they have the potential to influence programming decisions in favor of artists they collect or sell in order to inflate the price of their investment. Potential for the same conflict of interest to occur exists when an artist's gallery subsidizes production costs. In anticipation of profit from future sales, the commercial gallery is likely to encourage and eagerly finance capital-intensive art works, thereby yoking an artist into a Faustian transaction in which the subsidy must eventually be repaid as a loan, with the funds subtracted from the future sales of their work.

Whether or not the sale of the work produces revenue for artist or institution, W.A.G.E. Certification does not recognize the coverage of production costs as a form of compensation. To consider production as a monetizable investment would require addressing the second life of the work in the commercial marketplace, and as such would mean recognizing artistic labor as a form of commodity production, thus encouraging capital-intensive projects and their circulation within the speculative market. Instead, W.A.G.E. Certification locates itself within a services model, defining compensation on the basis of content or services provided.

To read the complete policy for W.A.G.E. Certification and to view the W.A.G.E. Fee Schedule please visit wageforwork.com.

30. Porgy

Written in November 1988 and previously unpublished.

I got plenty of nothing,[1] and nothing's plenty for me.[2]
— Porgy[3]

1.

This is not literally true. I have a secure and very satisfying non-art-related job that I wouldn't give up even if I could, and that allows me to live in the neighborhood of the standard of living to which I wish to become accustomed. This job also buys most of the materials for my artwork, in addition to providing some material for it. It doesn't provide enough money, of course. I have a lot of fancy, expensive ideas that I can't afford to realize, and I must be more thrifty and resourceful than I would like in realizing the ideas I can afford. And since it's a full-time job, finding time to do both it and my artwork is a *big* problem because it's not psychologically possible for me to give up doing either. Recently the peripheral demands and pressures of both jobs have begun to increase, and I've been spending most of my time frantically trying to find a way to continue doing both without reducing my creative involvement with either. I have anxiety attacks, don't sleep enough, often forget to eat, and don't see enough of my friends. I also get colds and the flu a lot.

On the other hand, I wouldn't actually realize most of the artwork I think about doing anyway. Although I get ideas almost continually, I ultimately reject most of them for reasons of quality. My natural rate of production, when I am not under pressure to produce artwork for shows, is relatively low—about three to six works per year. So far I've managed to maintain that.

I recently joined a gallery to help ease the administrative burden connected with my artwork, in the hope that this will give me more time to actually do my work. My dealer is someone I have known and respected for over twenty years and was the first person ever to actually show my work. This has led me to think *a lot* about the fact that although I have been exhibiting my work and have been professionally active in the field for over twenty years, I have never actually sold anything [Note: False! as of May 1989! Hurrah!].

2.

What I mean is that I'm actually rather proud and gratified at having managed to survive professionally as an artist without ever having sold anything. I've gotten a different kind of attention that is much more important to me. When a curator invites me to show, or a critic writes about my work, or an institution invites me to speak or participate on a panel or in a conference, they send me the message that they think my work is significant, and that motivates me to produce more of it. When a foundation awards me support, the main message it communicates to me is that my work is worth financial support *even though no one stands to make a profit on that work, or gain social status by acquiring it, as a result*. All of these expressions of support are essentially *disinterested* rewards. Obviously the money is extremely important because it buys time and materials. But the symbolic meaning of disinterested support in general is even more important. It reminds me that I am not alone in thinking my work worthwhile. And that gives me the courage to go on doing it (and to experience deep respect and admiration for those who like my work, and pity and disinterested concern for those who don't).

Art-market success by itself would have bought me time and materials, but it would not have conveyed to me that other people think my work is worthwhile. It would have conveyed to me that other people think my work is worth buying and selling and acquiring and displaying in their homes. In trying to comprehend the full significance for me of having joined a gallery, I find I feel very ambivalent about the very possibility of art market success. I worry that if I start getting financially rewarded for what I do, I'll start doing what financially rewards me rather than what I believe is worth doing. Even worse, I might come to believe that what is worth doing is what financially rewards me. That possibility really scares me, and I don't know that I would have the ego strength to withstand it.

I voluntarily withdrew from the market part of the art world when I was twenty-one. It was easy to do because I had never thought about market success as a professional goal and didn't like the effect of its proximity on my state of mind and creative processes. Perhaps I was just too young. One result of that decision is that I have focused my energy elsewhere, that is, on politically catalyzing the viewers of my work (yes! I actually believe art can do this). I don't mind producing work that most viewers find difficult, both in form and in content. I tell myself that self-awareness is hard to elicit, that real political and social change takes time, and that my work is, in effect, a test that many people can be expected to flunk.

Another result of having dismissed the possibility of art market success is that my social relations with most denizens of the art world are pretty good. I don't promote my work to dealers, collectors, critics, or curators when I encounter them. Usually we just gossip and party. I don't compete with artists who make a living from their work. We just hang out and talk about Big Ideas.

Cell phone image taken by Cameron Rowland sent via SMS to Carissa Rodriguez on 5/8/14; a detail from *The Probable Trust Registry*—a solo exhibition by Adrian Piper at Elizabeth Dee Gallery, New York, 3–31 May 2014.

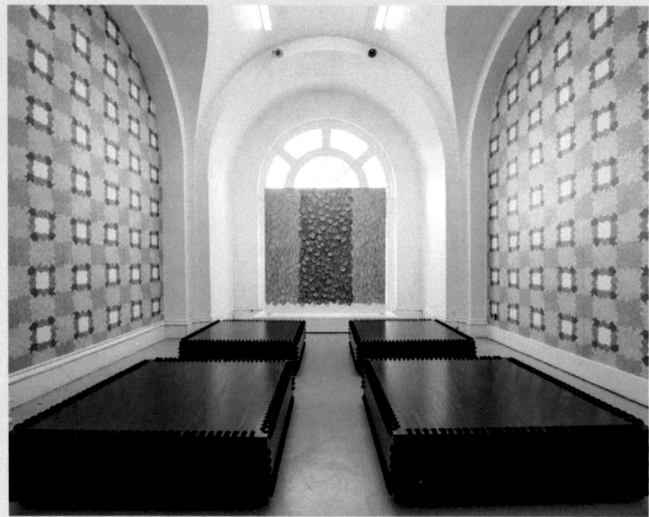

Jason Yates, *Master and Servant*, 2012.

Los Angeles, Saturday morning, 5 April 2014: we're in Jason Yates' apartment, sitting on stools at the breakfast bar. The apartment is almost entirely furnished with his art work: wall pieces and plinths papered with cross-hatched line drawings; black wooden boxes bound with black cord that function as beds, shelves and tables. Are these pieces sculpture or furniture? Scary or whimsical? The installation view from *Master and Servant* looks like the inside of a chapel...

: I picked that room because it was a meditative space. That's what I was interested in. The show was in Louisville, Kentucky and it opened in tandem with the Kentucky Derby.
    Hundreds of years ago my family lived in Kentucky, and they owned slaves. It was part of my history, and the history of that area. Now, *that's* something no one wanted to talk about.

: The beds are low to the ground, almost like caskets—

: In this piece, I was actually addressing the body, and the objectification of people. Most of the time I think power is an illusion, an idea that's imposed. It's a relationship. There's a sadomasochistic tension; roles people have agreed upon and are willing to play.

: *Master and Servant*...

: That's how power is formed. It's theatrical. We're setting up structures, and they become part of our fantasy, and it's almost like these relationships—we need them, we need to dominate or repress. It's kind of timeless. But if you get to the bottom of it, it's just a game, an illusion.

: And when people try to get out of that loop? There's another wall piece you made [*The Golden Road to Unlimited Devotion*, 2012]. It's orange, it looks like a Creamsicle.

: That's another way of looking at power... it's almost a flower child sentiment. The idea that, I'm going to transcend this.... But devotion is a form of submission, it's very extreme. I'm still trying to transcend the structure of perceived power.

: In this room, there's a tension between things.

: Yes, I'm talking about the value of painting versus the value of sculpture. I feel like, when we're dealing with sculpture, we're always dealing with bodies in conflict. Sculpture always operates within a physical space, whereas painting is seen as a higher form—

: Like the chakras: Body, low; brain, high. Avital Ronell talks about this mind/body split in *Stupidity*.

: Yeh, in that sense sculpture is stupid, it entails a struggle with your body. But, paradoxically it's a power form, historically preserved and consumed by the upper classes.

: And yet, when you make a bed or a table, the viewer is able to 'dominate' it, use the work in an active way.

: The Allen Jones BDSM sculptures from the late 1960s—

: They're a joke, sort of—

: Very submissive—

: The bed, I made that right after my divorce as a way of reclaiming power. After the loss of the family unit.... Because it looks super butch—

: —(laughs) A bachelor fetish. And that tension is what makes something art—

: Yeah, but there's this whole other aspect of this that fascinates me. Thinking about Brian Wilson, his whole downward spiral.... To drop out and escape is a whole different way to exercise power, to relinquish power completely.

Sculptural form—whether it has been hewn from a block, intricately cast, or wildly (mis) assembled—entails a basic trifecta of materiality, spatiality, and scale. Each aspect is a potential anchor or foothold where meaning might coalesce. Meanwhile, context reshapes the multiple meanings that emerge, as does every subjectivity that encounters the work. All of this necessarily has to do with the intersection of ambivalent, contradictory sets of power relations between maker and patron, an artifact's singularity and historical positioning, the artist's imagining of public reception and the actual circumstances of viewing and viewers, the art market and marketability, the demands of the present versus those of the future, the abstractness of conceptual notions of space, and the stark realities of premium realty. Sculpture doesn't usually go above the couch, though it might *be* the couch, and normally finds itself relegated to a space between materiality and meaning, where spatial utility is suspended. If only more such space existed! We grapple with sculpture rather than just look at it. The problem-relations are the conceptual materiality of sculpture. Sculpture, whether flimsy, weighty, imposing, slapstick, or absurd, involves a particular negotiation that wall-bound works don't, and a different threshold between subject and object than, say, installation or performance. One of the qualities of sculpture currently being explored is the possible slippage between these identities. It doesn't matter now if we are thinking of something that might have taken shape on an anarchist's office desk, has components ordered from the Internet, or emerged miraculously from a kiln or furnace. The dematerialization of much form and imagery in the digital information age has probably only heightened the longing for hand-managed material and a sculptural dialogue in a given space in a given time by embodied persons: emphasized by either the presence or absence of each. SculptureCenter's exhibition two years ago of sculptor Nairy Baghramian's *Retainer*, 2013, and the installation last spring of her *French Curve*, 2014, on the terrace of the Art Institute of Chicago, together with its flaccid indoor partner *Slip of the Tongue*, 2014, point directly to the power issues embedded in or shaping all sculpture. Though wildly associative of the body or, better, contraptions for articulating fleshed-out encounters in built space, her sculptures aren't *about* something else, rather they investigate the nature and tenets of sculpture itself. They ask: who gets to be and who wants to be big or small, permanent or impermanent, outside or inside, vertical or horizontal, contained or sprawling, taking up cultural space or retreating from it, refined or a mess, and equally importantly for whom? And is the architecture, institution, or gallery the foil, the frame, or the protective carry box?

Postwar art explored new ideas about materiality, production models, and value-adding judgments, but feminism remained at its fringes. Sculpture, perhaps even more diffidently (if that is possible) than the wallflower of painting, remained a mono-gendered domain. Perhaps only through the acknowledgment of power at play is emancipation possible.

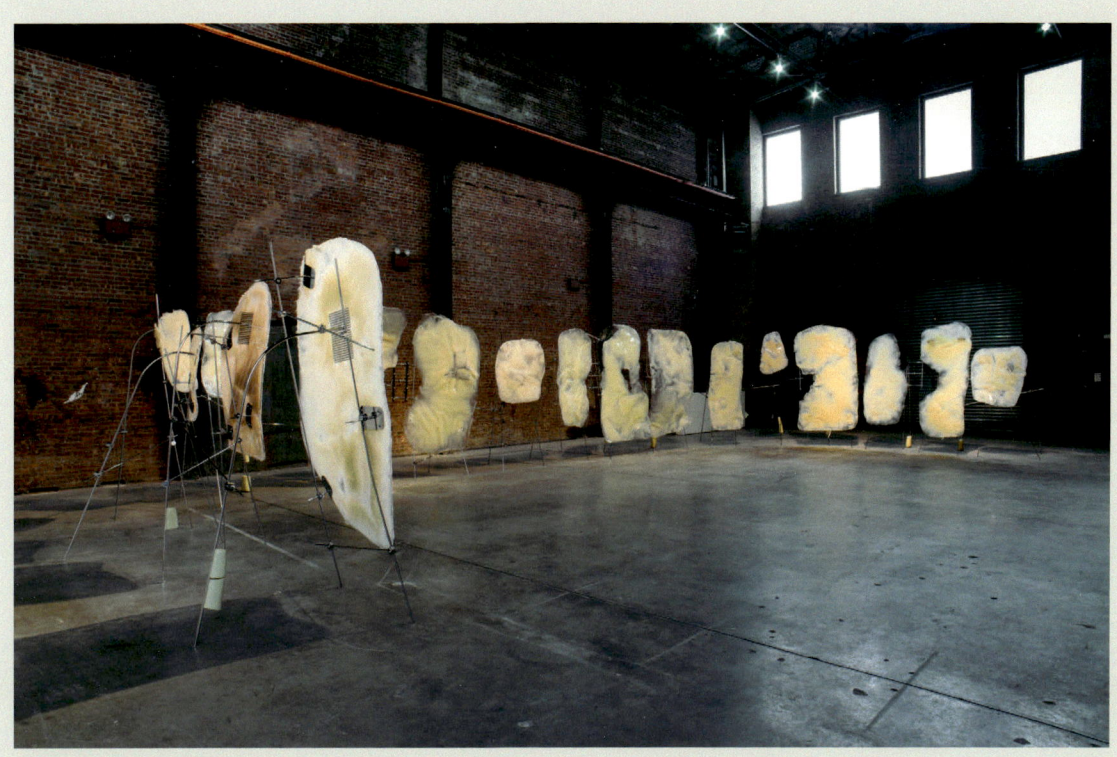

Nairy Baghramian, *RETAINER*, 2013.
Installation view at SculptureCenter, New York.
Photo: Jason Mandella.

In the early evening, you can often see a schoolchild poking her head through the kitchen window of a timber home on stilts by the water's edge. The air is heavy with the rich smells of cooking. The child knows that if she waits and bides her time, the grandmother who lives there is sure to reward her with pieces of crisp corn patties. The grandma has a soft spot for the motherless child, who is ravenous after having just arrived home from school.

Many decades pass, and her hair whitens to a shade similar to the grandmother's. The faces poking into the kitchen are those of stray dogs she has taken in from here and there. The dogs trail after the wafting aromas of cooking in a way that reminds her of her childhood. She has a soft spot for the dogs, as the grandma had toward her.

The child and the dogs share the position of "those who must be looked after", entitling them to special favors. We fail to lend adequate significance to the treats dispensed at the kitchen threshold, especially at a stage of life when the future seems infinite. The simple relationships are gradually transformed into old memories filed away on dusty shelves deep within our mental archives. They may never again intrude into our consciousness. We abandon our early bonds to embrace more complex and numerous relationships, leaving behind the position we occupied as children. We step from the verandah above the water onto a bigger stage.

We smile when we're complimented for earning the grades that make us the top scorer in a class of 30 students. We become part of a small clique eligible to enroll in an elite national university. As artists, we travel widely to see the world, questing for knowledge—concrete and abstract—for passion, and for understanding. We consent to a system of exchange, and we barter with our work. We play the game of ambition in response to social expectations. Our sense of rootedness, derived from the early bonds formed at the kitchen window, changes into something else.

Society and its traditions are the mechanisms through which we are controlled and our freedoms are defined. We often accuse our context and surroundings of imposing limitations, while we assert those of our characteristics that society lauds. This emphasizes our capitulation to a condition of being governed, as clear a pattern as the hammering of nails into a coffin, as loud as the repetitive dirge: "I who lie here, my life has past."

We allow ourselves to be governed; our daily lives, whatever their activities, are never free of negotiations with power. We switch sides often and easily. We are sometimes the keepers of power, and can establish the rules and define our relationship with other individuals and groups—those with whom we have affinity, and those with whom we do not. Power relations are always present in these relationships. One is either "inferior to", "superior to", or "equal to" the other. This dynamic is most fraught in our relationship with ourselves, in the inner conflict between our desire to preserve our privacy and individuality and our impulse to raise our stature in the eyes of others.

If art is a process in which potential is explored through the individual's emotion and intellect, then artists as a group are, by virtue of their production, practitioners of a method that avoids the ready subjugation to power: "For only if man does not repress the essential part of his self, only if he has become transparent to himself, and only if the different spheres of life have reached a fundamental integration, is spontaneous activity possible."[1]

The artistic ego is not different from any other—in the power relations of daily life, we too are sometimes on top, sometimes on the bottom. Regardless of these cycles, artists are first and foremost captive to the authority of the "ego of the self". According to Buddhism, the ego-centered faculty is considered "a mistake in intention and thought" that wields authority over truth.[2] Power manifests as a process that distorts the structure of ordinary life. The question arises: do we masochistically desire subjugation to a more powerful force, or can we escape from this prison by seeking help and empathy from the wielder of power?

We turned our backs on that kitchen window through which a grandmother used to pass us warm, crisp corn fritters. Our new—rootless—bonds underscore our insecurity, our weaknesses, our masochism, our sense of inferiority, and lead us to trust in power systems, such as those that organize religious or ideological communities. This faith increases our degeneration, desolation, and confusion. We were not warned that the self is the currency exchanged for the security of the group or belief system. Abstract values combine with brute fade. Consent is demanded for the compartmentalization and classification of protagonist and antagonist relationships. These dynamics are most clearly discerned in the private sector, where every element is enthralled by the power that can be gained in competition.

The passing of the delicious corn fritters to the small child by the grandmother's hands represents a different kind of power, what might be called inner power. This majestic relation is composed of duty, compassion, and affection, qualities that are often overlooked in the culture of capitalist exchange. Yet, while external power has a demonstrated capacity to suppress when it is wielded by individuals, organizations, institutions, or the popular imagination, this is not to say that inner power has the opposite effect. Inner power can burn just as greedily.

The "power of power" in both cases can distort the effort to assess its effects. In moral terms, the highest social esteem should be accorded to acts of duty and responsibility; instead, it is awarded to acts of magnificence. Success is defined by the value attributed to an act or work rather than its intrinsic substance. In the art world, a well-known work by a famous artist gains power from its social approval, regardless of whether or not it succeeds on critical grounds. Power can sometimes deceive us into accepting the superficial.

A Thai artist of an older generation has said:

According to my understanding, power is a static force that lies within us. What we notice is that the royal horse of King Taksin (figure from monument sculpted by Professor Silpa Pirasri, founder of the first fine arts university in Thailand) harbors immense strength.[3] But he is represented as a still figure. Without moving, he demonstrates a power that we imagine can be mobilized within seconds. Similarly, an industrial electrical transformer has the potential to generate massive amounts of energy purely from its internal mechanics.

We concur that power is a static and invisible force. In Thailand, "bodily power" (พลังกาย, pá-lang gaai) or "physical strength" (กำลังกาย, gam-lang gaai) is considered secondary to mental strength. The power of critical thinking, and especially that of creativity, has the highest value. Good art, which has these qualities embedded in it, has the potential to affect everything.

The episode that opened this narrative is repeated here:

Many decades pass, and her hair whitens to a shade similar to the grandmother's. The faces poking into the kitchen are those of stray dogs she has taken in from here and there. The dogs trail after the wafting aromas of cooking in a way that reminds her of her childhood. She has a soft spot for the dogs, as the grandma had toward her.

In *Thus Spake Zarathustra*, Nietzsche sizes up man's condition in a relevant way:

Ye constrain all things to flow towards you and into you, so that they shall flow back again out of your fountain as the gifts of your love.

Verily, an appropriator of all values must such bestowing love become; but healthy and holy, call I this selfishness.[4]

The child in our story has learned that the balance of power is neither stable nor permanent, and that the act of giving more often than not demands sacrifice, as does accepting. Because power circulates in relationships, and because relationships are unstable due to the dynamic of giving and taking, power is always in a state of tension.

"The man of knowledge must be able not only to love his enemies, but also to hate his friends."[5]

Contemporary art is not transparently representative of its era. Galleries select and define groupings of art and artists. Artists themselves look to these contextual constructs to situate their work and to gauge reactions to it. Often, power's primary value lies in its ability to be sensed, and this awareness sustains its momentum.

Given these ambiguities and evolutions, we ask, "What is power, and how can we recognize its moving parts?"

Translated by Nepal Asatthawasi

1   Fromm, Erich, *Escape from Freedom*, New York: Farrar and Rinehart, 1941, p. 258.
2   Attributed to Buddhadasa Bhikkhu (1906–1993), a famous and influential twentieth-century ascetic philosopher. Known as an innovative reinterpreter of Buddhist doctrine and Thai folk beliefs, Buddhadasa reformed conventional religious views in Thailand and abroad.
3   Taksin or the King of Thonburi (1734–1782), of Thai-Chinese heritage, was the only king of the Thonburi Kingdom. He was a leader in the liberation of Siam from Burmese occupation after the Second Fall of Ayutthaya in 1767 and the subsequent unification of Siam after its fragmentation under various warlords. He established the city of Thonburi, located across the Chaopraya River from modern Bangkok, as the new capital of Siam.
4   Nietzsche Friedrich Wilhelm, *Thus Spake Zarathustra*, trans. Thomas Common, New York: Cosimo, 2009, p. 48.
5   Nietzsche, *Thus Spake Zarathustra*, p. 50.

Contributors

Rossella Biscotti is an artist based in Amsterdam.

Gregg Bordowitz is an artist and writer based in New York City and Chicago.

Tom Burr is an artist based in New York City.

María del Carmen Carrión is an independent curator, critic, and Director of Public Programs & Research at Independent Curators International.

Heman Chong is an artist based in Singapore.

Dominic Eichler is a writer, former contributing editor of *frieze* magazine and cofounder of Silberkuppe, Berlin.

Malik Gaines is an artist and writer based in New York City.

Gordon Hall is an artist based in New York.

Anthea Hamilton is an artist based in London.

Jörg Heiser is a writer and co-editor of *frieze* based in Berlin.

Andria Hickey is the Associate Curator at the Public Art Fund.

Candice Hopkins is an independent curator and writer based in Albuquerque.

Chris Kraus is a writer and critic based in Los Angeles.

Margaret Lee is an artist based in New York City and co-founder of 47 Canal.

Jumana Manna is an artist based in Berlin.

Araya Rasdjarmrearnsook is an artist based in Chiang Mai.

Carissa Rodriguez is an artist based in New York City.

Katy Siegel is Professor of Art History at Hunter College and Chief Curator of the Hunter College Galleries.

Susanne Winterling is an artist based in Berlin and Oslo.

Emiliano Valdéz is Chief Curator of Museo de Arte Moderno Medellín (MAMM).

W.A.G.E. (Working Artists and the Greater Economy) is a New York-based activist group whose advocacy is currently focused on regulating the payment of artist fees by nonprofit art institutions and establishing a sustainable model for best practices between artists and the institutions that contract their labor.